The Couples Cure™ Book

Mastering the Art of Relationships
in 7 Easy Steps

The Couples Cure™ Book

Mastering the Art of Relationships
in 7 Easy Steps

by
Prestell Askia

THE COUPLES CURE™ BOOK

Mastering the Art of Relationships
In 7 Easy Steps

Copyright © 2015 by Prestell Askia. All rights reserved.

Library of Congress Control Number: 2015920649
ISBN-10: 0997429402
ISBN-13: 9780997429404

Published by:
10-10-10 Publishing
1-9225 Leslie St.
Richmond Hill
Ontario, Canada L4B 3H6
2nd Edition, Reprint: October 2016
Printed in the United States of America and Canada

Table of Contents

Foreword

Do you want to enhance and improve your current relationship? Have you and your partner considered how to rejuvenate your loving partnership? Is it time for a relationship renovation? If you are looking for fun and stress-free couple's solutions, this is the book for you. The Couples Cure™ Book, Mastering the Art of Relationships in 7 Easy Steps is filled with easy and dynamic partnership activities and exercises that can transform your relationship.

Prestell's magic formula, The Couples Cure™ System, is based on the wisdom and experience from people in healthy, happy, fulfilling relationships. She presents The Couples Cure™ System formula as pieces of a relationship puzzle. Each puzzle piece step in the formula is crafted from her conversation with hundreds of people who know what it takes to make their relationship work.

The fresh perspective to partnership challenges in *The Couples Cure™ Book, Mastering the Art of Relationships in 7 Easy Steps* will guide you through the steps to:

- Rediscover who you are and what you want from your relationship
- Address communication challenges and couples finances
- Redefine your relationship and cultivate the partnership you both deserve

I know the benefits of having a healthy, happy and fulfilling relationship. This book will teach you the secrets of happy couples. The 7 easy steps in the book show you not only *what to do*, but *how to do it*! By applying the fun and easy steps, tools and activities presented in this book, you too can reconnect the pieces of your relationship puzzle. You and your partner can have the relationship you want and deserve and change your life.

Raymond Aaron
New York Times Top 10 Best Selling Author

Acknowledgement

I am grateful for this incredible journey as an author. To my mother and father, Adelle Flagg Cowan and Preston Blanton, I am the living arrow sent forth from your loving bows. I am deeply grateful for your essence, your spirit and love.

To my husband Kemal, my children Shakir, Saleah, Danielle, Khalief and Tiffany, thank you for your unequivocal love and support. To my grandchildren, Savannah and Amayah, you are the angels of my heart; I love you more than words can express. To my siblings, Whilma, Reggie, Linda, Zelda, Janet, Joseph and Harold, I love you all. Wendell and Annie, we lost you too soon. To Diane and all my other FABNY members too numerous to mention, I love you. To Mom Mary Buell and Dad Robert Buell, it was mutual love at first sight.

To those of you in my village: Joyce Arps, Myesha Kershaw, Elizabeth Clarke, Richard Sampson, Leo Olson, Robert Lilje, Hilda Castaneda, Joanne Marshall-Mies, Claire Rosen, Velma Hendricks, John Tippit, Hiawatha Red Cloud Hawkes, Ann Joynt and Christina Hirose, I am thankful for your friendship, acceptance and unadulterated encouragement. To the many others who have graced my life for a reason, season and lifetime, I thank you for your presence.

Equally important are the hundreds of people who supported this labor of love, *The Couples Cure™ Book, Mastering the Art of Relationships in 7 Easy Steps*. You openly and honestly discussed your relationship experiences, wisdom and knowledge. Your conversations allowed me to capture the keys to healthy, happy, fulfilling relationships and share the wisdom with the world.

Introduction

The Couple's Cure™ Book, Mastering the Art of Relationships in 7 Easy Steps is the easy to read couples guide to fun and stress-free relationship solutions. This book is for partners in committed relationships who want to enhance or rejuvenate their partnership. The book is based on my personal conversations with hundreds of couples about their relationship challenges and how to address couples issues such as communications, sex and finances.

My magic formula, *The Couple's Cure™ System*, is presented throughout the book as pieces of a relationship puzzle. Each piece of the relationship puzzle provides a fresh perspective and approach to solve couples issues.

Every couple and partnership is unique. *The Couples Cure™* (**C**ouples **U**nique **R**elationship **E**xperience) *System* recognizes the multitude of relationship differences. Each chapter presents refreshing insight into solving partner's challenges with tools, activities and *how to* guidance. As the reader, you are introduced to Step 1, and provided the opportunity to indulge yourself and learn more about who you really are through the enlightening chapter on **Self Knowledge**. Next you open the door to the power of attitude and intention with **Mindset**. **Embracing Change** helps you appreciate that nothing ever stays the same, not you, your life, your environment and certainty not your relationship. These are all in a state of flux and constantly changing. Your task is to appreciate and value each occasion when you encounter change as a Rise of the Phoenix opportunity. You're also guided to learn the delicate nuances of Loving Communications, The Morse Code of Relationships in **The Message** Chapter. Ensuring both partners are recipients of sensual, intimate Win-Win Sex is the over aching message delivered in **The Platinum Sex Rule**. **Money Mates,** The Couples Guide to Easy Finances, helps to bring financial balance to your partnership. The chapter titled **Renegotiate** spells out the strategy and tactics for minor or major redesign, restructure or complete make over of your relationship, whenever it is Time For A Re-Do.

The last two chapters, Chapter 8 on **Letting Go** and Chapter 9 **Take Action Now**, complete the process. Chapter 8, **Letting Go** is a realistic, practical and civilized guide for those partners who ultimately end up severing their relationship. It is a progressive approach to separation or divorce. The breakup is the blessing for both partners; this tolerant approach enables both partners to leave with *No Regrets* while they *Appreciate The Experience* they shared together. The last chapter, **Take Action Now,** helps guide you and your partner, the architects of your relationship, through the transformation process as you begin to put the finishing touches on your newly designed partnership.

I'm The Couples Cure™ Lady. As a relationship coach, I've included an inquiry-based, thought-provoking approach to solicit answers to your relationship questions. This book is designed to be a self-help guide, reference book and dynamic tool for you and your partner to navigate the sometimes challenging waters of relationships ups and downs. The tools within offer a comprehensive guide of *what to do* and *how to do it* for relationships solutions.

What this book *Is...*

- The *Couples Cure™ Book, Mastering the Art of Relationships in 7 Easy Steps* has been written for committed couples who sincerely want to improve their relationship; equally important, these couples must be *willing* to do the necessary work to enhance their partnership. It provides the vehicle and methodology; it's up to the couple to develop and implement their own, unique resolution.

- This book is an easy to read couples handbook that provides the unique opportunity to re-do your relationship using fresh tools and activities that help you and your partner revitalize your relationship.

- This book is a personal coaching and self-help guide for partners who are not afraid to explore new and exciting experiential activities. These activities focus on improving relationships in key areas that make for healthy, happy partnerships, including self-knowledge, mindset, communications, change, respect, sex, money and renegotiations.

- This book includes couples experiential activities. As a life and relationship coach, I've included fun activities that systematically address you and your relationship from the **here and now** standpoint. My philosophy, while coaching both individuals and couples, has always been an attitude of acceptance. I provide the guidance to help you understand that: You can't change the past—what's done is done; however, you can affect the future. The question is: What are you going to do about it now?

- This book also provides website resources for PDF forms to supplement the examples contained in the book.

What This Book *Is Not*...

- This is not a dating book. It does not offer advice on how to meet, date or pick-up men or women.

- It is not a book that bashes or places the blame for relationship woes on one partner or the other; rather it challenges both partners in the relationship to reexamine what works, what does not work and make changes to salvage the partnership.

- This book is not designed to unearth any deep-seeded, hidden psychological issues you may have either now or in the past. This book will not probe into how you behaved as a child or who your parents were or were not. It focuses on your relationship – its current status and your vision for its future.

This book will teach you the secrets of happy couples. Although it's an easy read, don't be misled; this book is packed with shrewd, immediate and long-term partnership exercises. It will show you not only *what to do,* but *how to do it!* By applying the fun and easy tools and activities disclosed in these chapters, you too can reconnect the pieces of your relationship puzzle and transform your life!

Self Knowledge
Who the Heck Am I Anyway?

Chapter 1: Self Knowledge

Who The Heck Am I Anyway?

> *Self Knowledge is the beginning*
> *of self improvement...*
>
> Baltasar Gracián

Self Knowledge

Do you want more joy in your relationship? Do you desire more harmony and intimacy in your partnership? Do you crave loving connectivity and communication with that special person in your life? You're not alone. Every human being has the need and fundamental desire to improve or enhance their relationships.

Couples, partners and spouses in committed unions all experience challenges – some minor, some major – throughout the course of their relationship. As human beings, you and your partner, regardless of your current state of love or bliss, will undergo relationship challenges and issues. Equally important, you'll need to know how to quickly resolve those relationship issues and develop a repertoire of tools and skills to prevent them from reoccurring.

The first step in *The Couples Cure™ System* (Cure™ = **C**ouples **U**nique **R**elationship **E**xperience) and easiest way to prevent your relationship issues and problems from reoccurring is for you and your partner to become the conscientious architects of your future and your relationship. Now is the time to redesign the relationship you desire. To be clear, you have always been the architect of your life and your relationships. What you may or may not have realized is that you have always been a participating architect (albeit unconscious) in the development and status of your relationships.

Granted, there are other factors that contribute to your current relationship status; however, every decision you've made and each action you've taken have had a substantial effect, as an architectural building block, in laying the foundation for every aspect of your current status in life and your relationships. Likewise, as the participating architects, you and your partner have the power to resolve your issues and put the pieces of your relationship puzzle back together.

The solutions to your relationship puzzle already exist, and applying those remedies is easier than you might think. The solution to putting the puzzle back together lies within you!

The question you might ask is: *If the solution is already within me, why have there been few resolutions or only partial and temporary resolutions to my relationship issues prior to this? Or why don't I have the joy, harmony or intimacy that I desire in my relationship?* The answer is simple. You have not been ready or have not been willing to do the work to remedy your relationship woes. You weren't ready mentally and you weren't ready spiritually, and therefore you lack the motivation, willfulness and perseverance to make a permanent change as a participating architect of your relationship and life.

Have you ever wanted to lose weight and become more physically fit? Or, have you ever been a smoker and claimed that you wanted to stop smoking? Regardless of what you told everyone else and in spite of the gibberish you shared with other people, the reality is that you really didn't put forth the effort, but said you did. I know better. You see, I'm a former smoker myself and *alluded to the fact* that I wanted to stop smoking for years. But that too was malarkey. I was able to fool everyone else. The mouth said *Yes*, but the spirit and intention said *I don't think so -- at least not right now*. I knew deep down inside the pit of my stomach that I wasn't willing to do what it took to quit smoking. By the way, this nonsense went on for years.

Then one day I was hospitalized for minor surgery (although I didn't think it was minor at the time). And I decided, right then and there that I would stop smoking. That date was the 1st of October 2002; and I haven't had a cigarette since, nor have I even had a craving for a cigarette. Thank goodness! I realized as I was admitted to the hospital that the first step in changing behavior is to be perfectly honest with yourself and acknowledge whatever the real situation is. It is what it is! Deal with whatever the situation is and move on; then and only then can and will real changes occur. The same circumstances are true as it relates to your relationship. When you decide mentally and spiritually and you adopt the right mindset, then and only then can you become the architect of your relationship.

When you decide mentally and spiritually that you genuinely want to enhance, make changes or improve certain aspects of your life and/or relationships, you've made a huge decision. Congratulations! You've made a decision to shift your life's blueprint and internal paradigm. And you are to be highly commended. In making that decision, whether you know it or not, you've made a commitment to transform your life.

The first step in improving key aspects of your life via personal transformation is self-knowledge. Likewise, this is also the first step in mastering the art of your relationship. As you continue reading, you'll discover that *The Couples Cure™ Book, Mastering the Art of Relationships in 7 Easy Steps* and *The Couples Cure™ System* include self-knowledge exercises designed to help clarify who you are, define your values and support you as you become aware or examine your current beliefs. Self-knowledge is one of the most significant components on the path to self-improvement. It's also the gateway that will enable you to take the necessary steps to achieve the relationship you not only desire but deserve.

The term *Self Knowledge* is generally used to describe the *result of your human experiences* as you acquire an understanding and greater awareness of yourself. Quite often, self knowledge is characterized as an exercise in psychology, religious or spiritual study that enables you to delve into your innermost thoughts and subconscious mind to better understand yourself, your personality, characteristics and traits as you attempt to answer the centuries old questions: *Who am I? What am I like? What is my purpose? And what makes me happy?*

After you discover the answers to who you are, what your purpose is and what makes you happy, you'll be in prime position to achieve that great relationship. However, you must also establish a great relationship with yourself. To know who you are as an individual, you must clearly understand what makes you tick, what makes your spirit dance and your heart sing. Above all, you need to know what your values are, how you feel about relationships, the *must have* characteristics about your ideal partner, and what makes you happy.

Beliefs About Yourself

You're being forewarned and put on notice, that from this point on we're going to get up close and personal.

Are you up to the self-knowledge challenge? If your response is *Yes*, then let's continue. This chapter is all about you. It's designed to help you get to know, understand and reacquaint yourself with who you really are -- down to the molecular level.

If you are truly serious about re-establishing, re-learning or re-acquainting yourself with who you are, know that we're going to delve into your innermost thoughts, feelings and values. You'll answer questions about who you are, what you believe and how you feel about relationships. I'll challenge you to think about and understand why and how your innermost thoughts affect your behavior, your life, and your relationships—both with yourself and with others.

4

> *The thing that hath been, it is that which shall be; and that which is done is that which shall be done…*
>
> Ecclesiastes 1:9

This scripture refers to a prophetic truth: whatever experiences impacted our lives in the past will continue to impact and affect our lives in the future. This scripture is significant as you examine the state of your current relationship. It is essential to understand this biblical phrase because *that thing that hath been* refers to all the circumstances, conversations, and experiences that have had an impact on your belief system and behavior and are directly or indirectly attributable to your current behavior and the cause of your current situations. The *origin* of the *cause* is what you were exposed to during your early, childhood upbringing and occurrences. It is the sum total of all of your life experiences that dictate who you are and what you value today.

Again, where you are in life right now (your personality, relationships, finances, success, happiness, and general stance in life, etc.) are a direct result of your experiences, your thoughts, your beliefs and your actions. That being the case and as the chief decision-maker and architect in your life, it's safe to say that your life thus far is based on *your choices* and *your actions*.

The most efficient way to begin the process of understanding who you are is to accept responsibility for who you are right now. When you take responsibility for wherever you are in life and your current circumstances, you are well on your way to begin to shift your current life paradigm.

The first step in the journey to enhance your relationship is to unearth what and how you feel about yourself and your relationships.

While I am neither a psychologist nor a psychiatrist, what I know for sure is that human beings are both the architects and products of their thoughts and environments. As humans, we have the ability to rebuild, modify or change whatever is going on in our life. Equally important, as human beings, the capability exists to totally transform our lifestyle, relationships and experiences so that they are far more desirable.

Getting There From Here

Having established that you are an active participant in your own relationship, now is the time to open your mind and heart and take a close look at what *you* contribute to your relationship puzzle. This is neither the time nor place for you to indulge in the blame game and point fingers at your partner. You should use this opportunity to begin to change your life, modify and enhance your relationship. You can't change what happened in the past; however, you can take a stand, make the necessary adjustments and ask yourself a two-part question: **Where do I want to go from here and how do I get there?**

That change begins with a mere thought process. Your life will begin to change when you change the way you think. The next chapter on *Mindset,* explores just that, shifting your mind paradigm and adopting thought processes that will transform your life.

Albert Einstein said, *"It is harder to crack a prejudice than an atom."* When loosely translated, this means that our minds tend to be set in concrete until a major earth-shattering event causes us to look at a subject or issue differently. Otherwise, our thoughts are constantly driven back to what we first believed about ourselves, a person, an event, or an experience — *right, wrong, good, bad or indifferent.* Therefore, *how* you perceive yourself and the beliefs *you hold to be true* about yourself (whether or not they are accurate) are the perfect launch platform to address your personal assessment.

What Do You Value?

Before you can change anything about yourself and shift those mindset paradigms, you need to understand who you are and what you believe. The questions that follow will give you the opportunity to conduct a brief assessment about your beliefs — and become aware of *who you think you are* and *what you think about yourself.* Know that this chapter asks a number of thought-provoking questions to facilitate your understanding of who you truly are and those things that are of importance to you. On occasion, you may scratch your head, wonder and may not be able to answer some of the questions right away. No worries, put those questions aside for now. You can answer them later. Understand that this activity is designed to deepen your understanding of who you are. Let's begin with your values.

What Are Values?

Webster defines values as *"a principal, standard, or quality considered worthwhile or desirable."* Can you define your values? The exercise that follows will help you identify and clarify your personal values.

As a mentor, life coach and student of coaching for more than 30 years, I often use the most straightforward meaning and simplistic definition of values from Laura Whitworth, Henry Kimsey-House and Phil Sandahl. Their co-active coaching book, *Co-Active Coaching,* includes the following excerpts about values:

"*Values are not morals. There is no sense of morally right or wrong behavior here. Values are not about moral character or even ethical behavior, though living in a highly ethical way may be a value... Values are not principles, either, like self-government or a code of moral standards... Values are who we are. When we honor our values, there is a sense of internal "rightness" that has nothing to do with morality... Values are intangible. They are not something we do or have. Money, for example, is not a value, although the things you might do with money could be considered values: fun, creativity, peace of mind, service to others. Travel is not a value. Gardening is not a value. But both are examples of cherished activities that honor certain values, such as adventure, learning, nature, spirituality... When we live out our values, the various tones create a unique and blended harmony. When we are not living out our values, there is internal conflict dissonance.*"

Clarifying Your Values

The three-phase, fun exercise that follows was adapted from the Whitworth, Kinsey-House, and Sandahl coaching process. It was crafted to provide you with a snapshot of what your values are. It will also clarify those qualities you believe and embrace as worthwhile for your personal life and relationships.

Take out a piece of paper, 8.5" x 11", letter size. Draw two vertical lines, about 1 inch from each edge. (You should now have three columns on your paper: a one-inch left column, a 6 inch middle column and a one-inch right column.)

Phase 1. List your values.

Start with the center column and *list* your top 10 values. This initial step should be completed in about two-three minutes. Remember, values are typically one or two intangible words. *Values are not something we do or have.* Since many people struggle with identifying their values, below is a list of a several values that might help you identify your values.

Sample Values List		
Integrity	Spirituality	Tradition
Directness	Empowerment	Aesthetics
Productivity	Self-Expression	Risk Taking
Contribution	Creativity	Freedom to Choose
Excellence	Action	Vision
Leadership	Honesty	Authenticity
Harmony	Success	Performance
Peace	Accomplishment	Community
Trust	Adventure	Personal Power
Decisiveness	Humor	Acknowledgment

Phase 2 Priority rank your values.

In the column on the left, *rank* your values from highest to lowest based on their importance and priority (i.e. 1st, 2nd, 3rd, 4th, 5th through the 10th ranked value).

Phase 3. Assess and rate how you live your value.

In the right-hand column, assign each value a number to indicate the level you feel you *live and achieve* each of your values. The number 1 indicates that you truly live your value, all the time, unequivocally and without hesitation. At the other end of the spectrum, if you rarely live up to a value, your rating should be a 9 or 10, which indicates that you consider the value a priority but you rarely achieve living that value for one reason or another.

In Phase 3, the objective is for you to assess how well and how much you actively live out each value. Remember, values are neither right nor wrong; values are simply an indication of who we are right now. Phase 3 may be the most challenging phase of this exercise, because it also demands that you really think before you provide a response. This assessment can also be the most telling of the three phases. The Phase 3 assessment activity requires you to be brutally honest in assessing how and the frequency with which you achieve your values.

One of my coaching clients recently ranked honesty as top value. He then struggled with the assessment process. The reason for his struggle is that he highly valued honesty; yet, he reluctantly admitted that he frequently stretches the truth and often tells "little white lies" just to keep peace and avoid conflict with his partner. Consequently, his assessed score for living his honesty value was 8 out of a possible 10. My client's fi-nal score for living his value was low because he didn't walk the walk when it comes to honesty.

Another example would be *integrity*. You could rank integrity as 1, yet list your level of living and achieving that value as a 5. Why? The simple reason may be that you make commitments that you fail to honor, or you have difficulty with follow through. Consequently, you may only do what you commit to do about 50% of the time. Therefore, ask yourself: *Do I really live up to my own level of integrity?* Think about it. If you honestly accepted responsibility for the 50% deficit, the next question would be, *What am I going to do about it and how can I change that behavior?*

Did you include harmony, joy, authenticity and excellence on your list? If you included these values on your list, how well do you live these values in your relationship with yourself? An equally important question is: What is your level of assessment for these values in your relationship with your partner? And how well do you live up to each of these values in your relationship with your partner?

What did you learn from your values clarification exercise? How did you fare in the assessment of "how you live your values" activity? Were there any surprises? Are there areas in this values exercise that you have identified as a target for self-improvement?

Realizing Your Beliefs About Relationships

The next self knowledge awareness activity is designed to guide you through the process of *clarifying your beliefs about your relationships*. Take out another piece of paper and answer the following questions about your current or past intimate relationships and partnerships:

- What is the purpose of your relationships? Partnerships? Marriage?
- What is your belief about your own relationship(s)?
- What is your intent when you enter into a relationship with another person?
- Do you believe that you enter into relationships to satisfy your personal needs? Or to satisfy someone else's needs?
- How do you know when he/she is the one?
- Has your belief about your relationship changed over time? If so, how?
- Is there a reserved or protected part of you — perhaps who you really are or how much you love — that is never revealed to anyone because you are afraid to be hurt?
- How many serious relationships, partnerships, marriages and/or commitments have you had? How long did each last?
- Is companionship your primary reason for entering into a relationship?
- Is sex and physical fulfillment the basis for your relationships?
- Do you enter into relationships for money? Power? Status?

- Are you are afraid to be alone?
- Why do you want to be in a relationship?
- Are your relationships too much trouble or too much effort?

Your Love And Relationship L.I.S.T.

The next step is to make a list of the characteristics you want in a relationship. The theory that you can't and won't be happy unless you know what makes you happy will be applied here. The same is true for not knowing what you want in a partner. If you don't know the characteristics and traits you want in a partner, how can you expect to know the ideal partner. As you make your list, carefully consider the following L.I.S.T. features:

L = Love with your head in addition to your heart. What does a loving relationship look like to you? What does a loving relationship feel like to you?

I = Itemize and write your list in considerable detail. This list should be executed with pen and paper. This is not the time to keep the thoughts of your ideal relationship and partner in your head. When you gain clarity about what you want and need in a relationship and in a partner, the easier it will be to get that relationship.

S = Scrutinize and surgically examine your list, but don't over analyze. Understand and explore the why and why not a particular characteristic or trait is on your list.

T = Trust your instinct. Go with your gut. You know what works for you and what doesn't. This is not the time nor place to second-guess yourself.

Your actual list will be comprised of three fundamentally different elements.

Element 1. Must Have

Your *Must Have(s)* in your relationship are those elements that are absolutes. A *must-have* is not negotiable. A *must-have* is definitely a deal-breaker. Understand that your must-have characteristic is a mandatory component that is immutable; otherwise your relationship won't work. And the reason the must-have is mandatory is because it is consistent with your value system. As we've discussed before, if you, your behavior or your actions are not in alignment with your values, it is guaranteed that your relationship will not function at its highest capacity. These non-negotiable components in your relationship are critical to your relationship's survivability.

I've interviewed dozens of individuals who said, *If I had only known that he or she did this, had this kind of personality, wouldn't do that, I would have thought otherwise before entering into that relationship.* What's being said here is that there is an element of the relationship or individual partner that was contrary to their belief system and simply was not a healthy component for their relationship.

The topic of children is a classic example of a must-have for me. Prior to my marriage, if ever I had discussions with and became involved with an individual who did not want to have children, I would simply acknowledge his desires and respect his wishes for a childless relationship. I knew without hesitation that his desires for a childless relationship would be grounds for me to exit the relationship — pronto! Children (or the lack thereof) are a cardinal component of any serious relationship. This topic is not an attempt to convince anyone to the contrary.

Since I was a little girl, I've always known that I wanted to have children, barring any physical complications. It never ceases to amaze me the number of men and women that I've interviewed who never openly discussed the topic of having children prior to marriage. Then there is the case of the couple where one partner or the other may not want to have children. The other partner assumes that with time they'll change their mind, or eventually want to have children. One word of caution for both men and women: If an individual says he or she does not want to have children, accept that as the honest-to-goodness truth when they say it.

Element 2. Nice To Have

A *Nice to Have* characteristic that you want in a relationship would be a desire. A trait that falls into the *nice to have* category includes those characteristics that are wants, needs or desired elements of the relationship

A *nice to have*, is just that--it's a nice to have. It does not mean the relationship will not succeed or will not be harmonious if the nice to have is not present. A nice to have characteristic simply means that it could make the relationship more viable. On the other hand, there are numerous couples who have differences yet they have successful partnerships.

For example, one of my *nice to have* characteristics on my personal L.I.S.T. was to have the same spiritual upbringing. When I met my husband Kemal, I had no idea that he was born and bred in the Catholic Church. As a matter fact, he spent his entire kindergarten through 12th grade in Catholic School. My early childhood religious upbringing, on the other hand, was predominantly AME (African Methodists Episcopal) and Baptist. Despite the differences in our religious upbringing, when it came to raising our children, we both agreed that our children would be raised in a Christian home.

The key here is that a *nice to have* is just that. It is not necessarily a deal breaker and can be worked out with little or no difficulty. The crucial issue is to ensure that you know exactly where you stand and where your feelings lie as you make your L.I.S.T. of desired relationship characteristics.

Element 3. Doesn't Matter.

Your characteristics under the *Doesn't Matter* category are really self-explanatory. *Doesn't matter* implies that whatever the characteristic is one way or the other, it doesn't matter. As an example, the education level of your partner or whether he or she owns a home or rents an apartment may not matter to a young couple.

14

In evaluating relationship characteristics where you have identified that a quality or characteristic *doesn't matter* one way or the other, then it shouldn't matter what the issue is. Factors under the "doesn't matter" element are simply those elements that really don't matter one way or the other. These may or may not have a bearing on the relationship and in some instances could even enhance the overall traits and characteristics of the partnership.

Also, age may not matter one way or the other if the individual couple is indeed happy together. I've seen many May/December relationships where one spouse was older than the other that turned out to be quite healthy and harmonious. On the other hand, I've also seen situations where couples were very close in age and ended up divorcing or separating.

Here is a partial list of must-have, nice to have, and doesn't matter qualities and characteristics. There are hundreds of others. Which ones are significant to you?

Must Have	Nice To Have	Doesn't Matter
Honesty & Integrity	Desire for Children	Profession
Sense of Humor	Similar in Age	Ethnicity
Vision & Goals	Values Timeliness	Education
Good Communications	Similar Spiritual Beliefs	Owns Home or Rents
Not Abusive	Enjoys Travel	Age
Similar Money Values	Community Involvement	Previously Married
Family Oriented	Physically Active	Introvert/ Extravert

The answers to these questions are critical. Why? Because your responses will produce an awareness of your beliefs and behaviors concerning your relationships. Your responses also provide insight into the future nature of your relationships. In addition, your answers create a roadmap for where you've been in the relationship zone. If you're pleased with where you are, great! If you see room for improvement or see a need to repair or enhance your relationship, then now is the time to consider transformation of your beliefs, refocus your intentions and thereby, design the outcome of your relationships in the future.

I realize of course that you probably thought this was just another one of those self-help books that didn't really have substance, and more than likely, you certainly didn't expect to have to dig so deep within to discover your hidden beliefs. Well, it is what it is. To truly reflect on where you want to go and what you should do to achieve that quality relationship, you need to start somewhere. And I ask you again: *If not now, then when?* Believe me, there is no better time than the present.

For some of you the process of examining who you are, what you stand for, what your purposes are, and what is meaningful to you may be a first-time experience. I also realize that it may be a very challenging effort for you to undergo this process of learning about who you really are and may be a bit daunting. However, rest assured that when you find out who you are, what your values are, and what you stand for, you will come out on the other side of this process a stronger and more knowledgeable person than you've ever been before.

This self-examination also will set you free from simply going along with your existing program, whatever that happens to be. When you begin to learn and understand who you are, whether you know it or not, you become self-empowered. Knowledge is power! These self-exploration exercises will enable you to become aware, understand and know who you truly are. This process will also enable you to identify what no longer serves you. And finally these processes will enable you to identify those values that you are currently living versus those values that you identify as priorities yet you're not in harmony with nor living those values.

16

Finally, having learned about and explored this whole new you, now is the time to take an assessment and embrace those elements of your personality that you enjoy and love. Now is the time to make up your mind and deal with those elements that you feel are not what you want to be or have. Now is the time to begin your transformation and make the decision to change those aspects of who you are. When you change the way you think, *things you see begin to change.*

Relationship Principle:

Your current life and affairs are based on your prior choices and behaviors. Your future is also based on your decisions and actions, so choose wisely to get different results.

Prestell Askia

Mastering The Art Of Self-Knowledge

Question:

Why is it important to learn about myself?

Answer:

Knowledge is power. Self-knowledge fosters self-confidence. When you know who you are, what you want out of life, what your values are, and you can express them accordingly, you become a much more powerful individual. When you increase your self-confidence, you become much more appealing as a person and you are able to bring so much more to your relationship.

Self knowledge also allows you to know why you do the things you do. It enhances your understanding of your values and why you act as you do.

You know that your values and your beliefs dictate your behavior and your actions. And your actions and choices have been the drivers of where you are right now in life. Finally, self-knowledge is your platform of understanding that you can use to begin to change your life and your relationships.

Self Knowledge Is The Key

Self-knowledge is the key to understanding myself, I and me.
To know, to grow and establish internal validity,
I must first seek and become aware of what constitutes the me.

If I'm not pleased with what I see in my life
And all about is unstable, distraught and without vision or sight,
When the tolerance of mediocrity is an unacceptable plight,
I know then and therefore that change begins with my personal insight.

Then and only then can I present my authentic self,
Knowing that I am at my very best;
I grow and expand the true me,
I discard what no longer serves and retain all the rest.

So my personal commitment from this day and beyond
Is to multiply my self-knowledge, edification and personal self-bond.

Prestell Askia

Now that you've had an opportunity to complete the first step in your relationship puzzle and put *The Couples Cure*^{TM} *System* to work, you're on your way to mastering the art of relationships.

In this chapter, you have clarified your values, completed your relationship LIST and described your beliefs about relationships. In the next chapter, **Mindset**, you'll learn about the significance of your mindset and attitude and how that particular aspect of your personality drives everything you do.

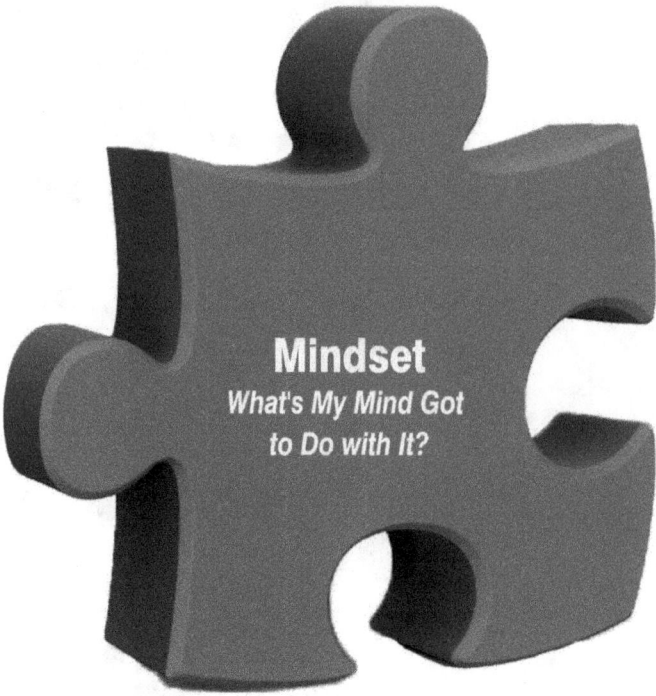

Mindset
*What's My Mind Got
to Do with It?*

Chapter 2: Mindset

What's My Mind Got To Do With It?

> *It's your attitude, not your aptitude,*
> *that determines your altitude.*
>
> Zig Ziglar

The Source

Step 2 in *The Couples Cure™ Book, Mastering the Art of Relationships in 7 Easy Steps* and *The Couples Cure™ System* of learning to master the art of relationships is to *adjust your mindset*. What's your mindset got to do with it, you ask? Everything! Your mindset has everything to do with everything and everything you're involved with — your thoughts about yourself, your family and relationships, your business and professional success — virtually all that you touch. In this context, your mindset is the *Source* or the "cause," the "basis," the very "foundation" from which all else flows.

This chapter directs the focus to understanding what your mindset is, the significance of having the right mindset for your individual situation, and how to develop and keep the right mindset.

The term mindset is defined as the source, the ideas and beliefs that affect your attitude. Your mindset is your personal view and the approach you use to address a given situation or anything in your life. Your mindset is the platform or launch-pad from which everything you do is initiated. What's more, your mindset is a mental attitude or disposition that determines your responses to and *interpretations of* situations. Your mindset is often referred to as your state of mind.

The state of your mindset determines the outcome of everything you do. Your mindset is the source or internal GPS within you that establishes the mental attitude, strength and stamina you need to engage in and achieve, whatever you want to do. The proper mindset is essential for you to move forward. Your mindset determines the "win from within" strategy.

It matters not whether you are an athlete, physician, homemaker, businessperson, florist or any profession in between. The principles of having the right mindset are all the same. Your mindset governs your willingness, your attitude, the commitment level of your belief, the difference between hoping and knowing, and ultimately how you respond to a given situation. The old adage, *"It's not what happens in life, rather how you respond to those situations that determines the quality of your life."* This is certainly true when it comes to your relationships and how your life unfolds.

Your Mindset Affects Your Future

There are several necessary mindset principles that you should adopt when you are ready to transition to a new mindset and way of life and, ultimately position yourself to receive the relationship you deserve.

A working principle is to establish and maintain a success conscious mindset. So how do you do that? What are the requirements? Will I need special training or to attend classes to adjust my mindset?

When you set a goal or make your mind up to change something in your life, you are either working toward that goal or working against that goal. There is no middle ground. Everything you do will either reinforce and support your life or work against it. Your life does not stand still. As human beings, our life continually evolves. Nothing in the human world ever stands still.

Famed author Napoleon Hill so eloquently depicts his definition of mindset in his book *Think and Grow Rich,* when he says, *"You're either success conscious or failure conscious." "You're either working toward your goal or against your goal."* When you establish that mindset, you must recognize and know when your mindset, your thoughts, and behaviors are working for or against your target goal. In your case the goal is to have a meaningful relationship.

The significant factor here is to recognize that you are either on the side of the "for" fence or the "against" fence. Because the mind is so powerful, quite often you do not recognize the fact that you allow yourself to slip into a success-failure consciousness mode.

Again I quote Napoleon Hill's inspirational classic, where he says, *"Failure comes to those who indifferently allow themselves to become failure conscious."* The message of his book is to help all who seek to learn the art of changing minds from failure consciousness to success consciousness.

Relationship Paradigm Shift

Everything changes. Nothing ever stays the same. In order to grow in your relationship and get the relationship you desire, you must be willing to modify your behavior. In modifying your behavior, you begin to change the dynamics of your relationship and the culture you and your partner have established for the relationship. Yes, every relationship, including yours, has a culture. Just as every country, city, corporate organization, military unit, family and household, you and your partner have also established a relationship culture. To improve that relationship, you must shift your relationship paradigm, ultimately changing the culture of your relationship. The Webster definition of a paradigm is *a distinct concept or thought pattern.* Another way to explain how to shift your relationship culture is for you and your partner to modify or change your relationship behavior.

This chapter will focus on shifting your mindset paradigm from whatever it has been to being success conscious. Modifying your thought processes takes practice. Shifting your mindset paradigm requires consistency and determination.

Squeezing The Tube

When my husband and I first married in 1984, I had the most difficult time with several of his habits. Back then, chances are I would've said that my husband's habits just didn't work for me. Or, as many of my sisters have been known to say, *"He got on my last nerve!"*

For the life of me, I could not understand why Kemal had no clue as to how to use a toothpaste tube. It was a simple tube of toothpaste, for crying out loud! What was the big deal? Everyone knows that you always squeeze toothpaste from the bottom. Surely every child was taught that as s/he grew up. The rationale was simple. In the late 1800s toothpaste tubes were made from metal until shortly after the Second World War when toothpaste tubes were made from a combination of both metal and plastic. And in the 1960s the manufacturers began switching from the combined metal and plastic to all plastic. Every child in my neighborhood knew that you always squeeze the toothpaste tube from the bottom. Squeezing from bottom preserved the tube of toothpaste and ensured that you got all of the toothpaste out. Otherwise the metal would buckle, and prevent one from getting all the toothpaste from the tube.

I come from a family with six siblings. We were not poor – or so I thought at the time – because everyone in the neighborhood was in the same boat and we were happy, well fed, and were none the wiser. My mother always made reference to conserving the toothpaste because there were so many of us in the family and she simply wanted to ensure that any tube of toothpaste went as far as possible.

The other habit I discovered that was well ingrained in my husband was this thing he did with the newspaper. He had this horrific habit. Wherever he read the paper, there it stayed. If he read the paper in the bedroom, at the kitchen table, in the bathroom or on the family room floor, he left the paper wherever he read it. To make matters worse, he didn't even bother to leave the newspapers neatly stacked.

Wherever he finished reading the paper is where he left it. I kid you not, this business of leaving the newspapers whenever, wherever he finished reading them used to drive me bananas.

I was so frustrated in the beginning of our marriage, I would ask him time and time again to please squeeze the toothpaste from the bottom and pick up his newspapers and either trash them or put them in a neatly organized spot.

These two scenarios – the toothpaste and the newspapers situations – occurred quite some time ago, at the beginning of our marriage. What I know now and didn't know then, was that the issues were not with my husband, but rather with my own perspective. I failed to realize that I had grown up with the understanding that there was only one way to do things. And that way, of course, was my way. That was understandable; it was all that I knew at the time. What I mistook for a bad habit wasn't bad at all. It was *my* interpretation of the situation and what occurred, and how I behaved and reacted to those circumstances that made all the difference in the quality of our relationship. It was my mindset that needed to be adjusted.

One of the major turning points in our early relationship occurred when I decided to take a close look at my husband's newspaper and toothpaste lifestyle behaviors. When I put those two habits and lifestyle behaviors in perspective, it made all the difference in the world.

Wearing my analytical hat, I decided to take inventory of all the things my husband did. I started with the fact that my husband has been a consummate provider for our entire marriage. We have three children, all of whom have college degrees and our eldest son has a Master's degree. In 30 years of marriage I have never gone to bed without him cleaning the kitchen and doing the dishes. Never once have I awakened to a dirty kitchen. I'm generally the first one up in the morning, and I do not like coming downstairs to have to navigate my way through dirty dishes in the sink in order to make coffee. He does the dishes whether it's just the two of us, our family, or an elaborate Thanksgiving dinner where we have some 32 family members for a traditional turkey feast. Our evening dishes are always done before we go upstairs to retire for the evening -- every single night!

Never once in our entire marriage has he ever left his clothes lying around on the floor, in the chair, or elsewhere in our bedroom. Doesn't matter whether he wears his three-piece business suit, his casual clothes, or he's just returned from jogging in his sweats and sneaks, he always, always, always puts his clothes away, in the clothes hamper or hangs them up immediately. I, on the other hand, have been known to leave my clothes hanging on our rocking chair or one of the other chairs in our bedroom. My clothes eventually managed to get returned to their rightful location. Never once have I *ever* had to pick up behind or after my husband Kemal.

You may ask why that's important and why this topic of habits and behaviors is included in the chapter on mindset. When I adjusted my mindset, my perspective and the entire situation changed. Needless to say, I am forever grateful to my mother-in-law, Mrs. Ida Halliburton Pickney, for the amazing job she did in raising her son, my husband.

Adjust Your Mindset And Attitude

Your mind commences the mindset adjustment process when you accept full responsibility for your life. Your mindset and the life you currently have will change when you embrace and begin to practice the following mindset principles:

- **You Co-Create Your Life**. Accept and understand the power you possess in the execution of your life. As a human being you can change the course and direction of your life as well as your relationship. You have far greater power than you could ever imagine and it all has to do with your mindset and the execution of your intentions. You can change what would've been a bad day to a good day. You can change a set of circumstances from a sad situation to a tolerable situation and ultimately to a happy situation.

One day about 15 years ago I called my brother Harold. When I asked him how he was, he said it was going to be a bad day. I asked him what the problem was. He responded by saying, *"It's going to be a bad day, I got up on the wrong side of the bed..."*

So I asked him, **"***Is there anything else that would cause you to feel or think that you're going to have a bad day?***"** *"No"* he said, *"I just got out of bed on the wrong side; and so, **I know I'm going to have a bad day.***"*

Then, I said to Harold, *"For crying out loud, Dude, if you get out of bed on the wrong side and it's going to make you feel bad, then for heaven sakes get back in the bed and get out of the bed on the other side."*

The moral of this story is that it really is as simple as mind over matter. Because you think something is going to be or turn out bad, it's almost guaranteed that it will.

No doubt you've heard the stories about the conspiracy of the universe and how the universe works to conspire with your thought process. Take for example the person who says, *"I can't do it."* Or the one who says, *"I can do it."* The Universe simply says *"Okay."* The Universe does not judge; it does not understand right or wrong, good or bad. The Universe will never attempt to change your mind. The Universe simply delivers. It delivers whatever it is you believe, think and feel.

- **Maintain A Spirit Of Willingness.** It is imperative to maintain a disposition of willingness. A willingness disposition is an attitude that says you can do it. It's an attitude you must embrace when you make a conscientious choice to do something. I make the distinction between willingness and willpower. Willpower implies an inside, perhaps hard-core "internal force" to be maintained. Quite the contrary with a willful spirit; a willful spirit denotes a character that is willing to do a task, but without force. It is void of power which requires *overcoming* a state of mind. A willingness disposition suggests that you are willing to do and maintain a particular spirit, without the negative connotation of forcing yourself to do a certain thing or be a certain way.

- **Determination**. Recall the story from your childhood nursery rhymes, *The Little Engine That Could*? My granddaughter is six years of age and I frequently make reference to this childhood book and the power of optimism.

The basic theme of the Little Engine story is the same--a train is stranded and is unable to find an engine willing to take it over a difficult hill to its destination. However, the little blue engine is willing to try and, while repeating the mantra *"I think I can, I think I can,"* overcomes what seems to be an impossible task.

There are times when it's easy to fall into old habits.

I thoroughly enjoy aqua aerobics classes. My daily routine for the past three years, includes going to the gym five sometimes six days per week for aqua aerobics classes. About 95% of the time I am all in. There's no doubt about what I need to do. What I want to do. What I choose to do. However there are times when I wake up in the morning and all I can do is get out of bed, let alone go to the gym. What I know for sure is that those are the days when I make a concerted, conscientious effort because of my determination to go to the gym. Those are the days that I feel 110% better. Not only do I feel better, but there is something that occurs within on a spiritual level. That internal spiritual feeling is the added boost that makes me feel even better.

This determination scenario reminds me of a favorite saying from a New York Times best-selling author, Lisa Nichols. Ms. Nichols' book, *No Matter What*, articulates her mantra, *no matter what,* as the key to overcoming any obstacle in your life. Her book is a powerful delivery of personal attestation along with every day principles that address the nine steps to living the life you love. If you've not read Lisa's book, by all means do so.

- **Mindfulness.** Mindfulness denotes the frequent and constant refocus of you mind, thought processes and thinking patterns so as to maintain and pay complete attention and awareness to the present experience, without judgment nor thoughts of past experiences or future occurrences. The principle of mindfulness has been around for quite some time and is believed to have originated in the Eastern meditation practices. The purpose it serves in the process of establishing the correct mindset is to ensure that the focus of your attention is on what is going on today, right here in the here and now.

- **Passion And Enthusiasm.** Passion and enthusiasm are critical in the resolution of your relationship issues and challenges. Far too often passion and enthusiasm are confused with busywork.

- **Commitment**. Commitment requires a willingness to pledge, dedication, and obligation of the time, effort and energy required to bring your relationship to where you want it to be. If you're not willing to commit and if you think that people don't see through your falsehoods and pretending, your relationship is not going to work.

What most don't realize is that karma plays a major role in relationships. How can you expect your partner to see your way of thinking and understand what your desires are if you're not willing to reciprocate and do the same? You cannot expect your partner to acquiesce and work with you when you are not truthful. You cannot expect your partner to work toward improving the relationship if you are unwilling to do the work yourself. Commitment takes effort. Once you both commit to transform your relationship and continue to work toward that goal, the Universe will conspire and support the effort and the results will be amazing.

Embracing and keeping a healthy, positive mindset is akin to replacing an old habit with a better, newer habit. Think about the process of losing weight, implementing a new physical exercise program or changing your eating patterns. Sometimes it gets downright tough. This new process of maintaining a positive mindset is like developing new muscles – it takes practice and consistency. New habits take determination. New habits require a willingness to stick with the program. Even though you may fall off the wagon, the key to achievement and long-term happiness and success is to get right back on that course of action without judging yourself or your partner.

Adopting The Couples Positive Mindset

The *Mindset Transformation Tool*, which follows, was developed for *The Couples Cure™ System* to assist you in adopting and maintaining the right mindset.

The column on the left of the tool, *Your Current Mindset and Challenges*, includes those less than desirable thoughts, attitudes and mindset that you may currently hold. The column on the right, *The Couples Cure™ System Positive Mindset*, represents the kind of mindset you want to embrace and adopt. In doing so, watch the change in behavior of your spouse or partner.

The Couples Cure™ System
Mindset Transformation Tool

Your Current Mindset Challenge & Thoughts	The Couples Cure™ System Positive Mindset
Blame Someone Else	Accept Responsibility
Apprehensive	Confident
Unwilling	Willingness
Apathetic	Enthusiastic
Non-committal	Committed
Skeptical	Convinced
Vacillate	Determined
Give Up	Persevere
Distrust	Faith
Can't	Can & Will

You are responsible to initiate the transformation of your mindset. You and only you can alter your thought patterns when you become aware that your source or mindset determines your happiness and well being.

Embracing Change
The Rise of the Phoenix
Opportunity

Chapter 3: Embracing Change

Rise Of The Phoenix Opportunity

> *The secret to change is to focus all of your energy,*
> *not on fighting the old, but on building the new.*
>
> Socrates

Change Is Constant

Step 3 in *The Couples Cure™ Book, Mastering the Art of Relationships in 7 Easy Steps* is based on conversations about change. I knew instinctively about what appears to be a human preoccupation with and reluctance to change. None-the-less, I was overwhelmed to learn that individuals and couples don't realize the significance of change in their lives. Far too often as I addressed this aspect of the relationship puzzle, I heard about changing circumstances from happily married individuals and those who divorced or separated due to the changes that occurred in their lives and their partner's life. Take note: It's *not only the change* that occurred that caused the rift between the partners. My discussions with couples revealed that a significant number of savvy couples and individuals confessed that *their own inability* to deal with and/or see these changes occurring were the primary cause for the severed relationships.

As I delved into the nature of their reticence about discussing change, I discovered the numbers of people who are reluctant to accept change. They were candidly outspoken about their preference to not be involved with any kind of change. I was stunned. I had difficulty believing that mature adults were unwilling to change or accept change in their partners. They claimed: *"After all, life was just fine before the change."* *"Leave well enough alone. No need to modify anything; we've been doing it this way for years."*

What was most interesting in these discussions was the manner in which the process of changing situations and circumstances surfaced in our discussion. For example, what I heard were statements of resentment toward changes that occurred in education levels, weight gain as well as weight loss, professional achievements and lack of career motivation to name a few. Some of the actual conversations about change continued with statements such as, *"After she went back to school and got her advanced degree, she no longer felt I was adequate as a partner."* I also heard comments like: *"She's changed; she no longer finds me desirable, and yet I'm the same man I've always been"* and *"I may have put on a few pounds here and there, but I'm still the same person."* Or, *"Once he started to climb the corporate ladder, he didn't feel I was the cute, little eye candy that I was when we first married."* Lastly, a number of couples addressed their partner's changed behavior, commenting that: *"Since he's taken that new spirituality class... Since she started working out at the gym... Since he read the new best seller about buying and selling real estate, he's changed."* So you fill in the blank about change. You get the message!

After digesting the barrage of comments about change, several questions come to mind. As you think about past relationships and your current relationship, recall the circumstances about the changes you experienced. Now, ask yourself: Was it the <u>change</u> or was it <u>your inability</u> to deal with the change? What role did you play in the change process?

The logical and necessary third step in *The Couples Cure™ Book, Mastering the Art of Relationships in 7 Easy Steps* is to prepare yourself for change — a change in yourself, a change in your relationship and a change in your life. Decidedly, the secret to change is to not only accept change, but to *embrace* change. Ask yourself the following questions about embracing change:

1. Are there circumstances or conditions relating to changes in my relationship behavior that could be improved?

2. Do I on occasion place blame on my partner for changes that occur in our partnership even though my partner may not be at fault?

3. Am I willing to make changes in my own lifestyle if it means more happiness, success and balance in my relationship?

If you answered *No* to any of the three questions above, stop reading right now and give this book to someone who really wants to experience joy and fulfillment in their life. With a *No* answer, you send a clear signal that you want and choose to remain stagnant in life; you choose to continue on your same path. There's an old saying, *"If you keep doing the same things you've been doing, you're going to keep getting the same things you've been getting."* My guidance to you is to not waste your time; you're either extremely content with your current circumstances or you've made a conscientious decision to remain stagnant. Either way, you should immediately gift this book to a friend, family member, or partner who is truly interested in improving the quality of their life and relationships.

You Are The Critical Mass

If, however, you answered *Yes* to all three questions, then continue reading. You're ready for Step 3 in *The Couples Cure™ System*. You're the type of person this book was designed to help. You're willing to put forth effort and you've started taking steps to change or enhance some aspects of your life. You're ready to make a change.

Get prepared to embrace change. You also need to be ready *to be* the change. If you are skimming this book or happen to be a speed reader, I urge you to go back and reread the prior sentence. Did you notice that "to be" was italicized? Perhaps not. So, let me restate this ever so critical component that is required to master the art of your relationship and your life. *To be the change* is the critical mass component that is required to change your life and relationships.

A physics lesson this is not. Albeit using the term critical mass in the context of amplifying the significance of your mindset and your commitment *is* the subject of this current discussion. Your decision to be the change agent in initiating a transformation that redirects your future is most worthy of a little physics discussion here. Critical mass is the least amount of fission matter required to set off a nuclear chain reaction. Fission matter, namely the atom, is the tiniest element required to cause movement or change. In simpler terms and to bring the discussion home to relationships, your positive mindset and your willingness *to be the change* are the critical mass and minimum elements required to begin to make a change and see the chain reaction of modifications in your life.

Change is in fact a matter of physics. Webster's simplistic definition says that, *"Physics is the science of **matter & energy** and the **interaction** between them."* Other uncomplicated definitions include the results of physics as: change and transformation, cause and effect, action and reaction, and input and output. And finally, if nothing changes, nothing changes.

Change is the one element in life that remains consistent. Everything changes -- constantly. The more easily you accept and invite change into your life, the happier you will be. Think about it. The more you resist making adjustments in your own personal behavior, the more difficult it is to expect and invite healthy, happy changes into your relationship. Therefore, consider yourself the critical mass in making changes for the better in your relationship.

Be realistic...you can't prevent change. Change is going to happen. Ideally, you'll want to initiate, accept, manage, and ultimately embrace change. Embracing change is the mature and wholesome road to take when dealing with change. Surely you recognize that it is an uphill battle if not an impossible pursuit for you to long for everything in your life to remain as it is. Change is inevitable; the sooner you accept and embrace the fact that change is inescapable, the easier your life and relationships will become.

Change And The Unchangeable

Change is inevitable. The question is: Why isn't change more readily accepted? And, why do people have such difficulty embracing changes? The answer is best described in eight words: **fear and the inability to control the unknown**. Fear, lack of control, panic, anger, chaos, hopelessness, disorder, emotions, hurt — all of these emotions make us vulnerable and apprehensive about change.

Everything and everybody changes. Everyone! Period! So what makes you think you're not going to change and that your personal relationships will forever remain the same? Everything changes. Everyone changes. Consider some of the changes that have occurred in the United States and in the world. Also, think about your own personal changes and transitions.

Give thought to the evolution of time and changes that have taken place. The development of the wheel, the discovery of fire, the evolution of western world are all major changes that impact our lives today. Consider also the significant changes in the United States in the last century — the emancipation of slaves, women's right to vote, industrial revolution, invention of the airplane, indoor plumbing (Thank goodness for that invention!), electricity, telephones, and let us not forget computers, cell phones and iPods. Just to bring change into perspective, when I was a child which really wasn't that long ago, a mouse was a small, grayish looking rodent with a long, hairless, tail, that sometimes nested in the garbage or was lodged between the walls. It was typically caught with a mouse trap.

What about your own personal experience with change? In spite of your reluctance, consider the transitions that have occurred in your own life. Depending on your age, think about all the changes you've undergone in your *cradle to grave* process. As a human being, you've certainly aged, and undergone physical, social, and psychological changes during your human life-cycle development. Marriage or personal commitment to your partner, major moves across the country and across town, the death of a parent or child, changing jobs, changing companies, changing positions — all of these were changes that occurred and will continue to happen. As you look back on some of the transitions in your life, note that time has healed a number of wounds and made adjusting significantly easier. So get used to change. Otherwise the world and all your personal relationships will suffer because you're not willing to be flexible enough to work with change.

One of my live training workshops is *Embracing Change.* This workshop has been presented to thousands of people throughout the United States. Our *Embracing Change Workshop* uses *Who Moved My Cheese,* by Spencer Johnson, M.D., a primer to help workshop participants understand the significance of welcoming change into their lives and the consequences encountered when they resist change. The book's subtitle, *A-MaZing Way To Deal with Change in Your Work and In Your Life,* explains the simple parable that reveals profound truths about changes. The book is about four characters who encounter unexpected change and how each of the characters handles the constantly moving environments and shifting personalities in their daily lives. It is a simple, easy to read book that clearly provides tremendous insight into not only dealing with change but embracing change.

The thought of change for some people is difficult enough. And now you're being tasked to not only accept change but to embrace it. Difficult as it may seem, this is the beginning of the rest of your life. When you change your attitude and reluctance to welcome change to embracing change, I guarantee your life and relationships will show significant transformation.

Knowledge Is Power

Knowledge is power. Questions that stimulate your thought processes and ultimately reveal knowledge and awareness about you are a powerful process. In the first chapter, **Self Knowledge**, you embarked upon the **Who the heck am I anyway?** quest. The purpose of self knowledge is to learn all about yourself. If you took those fun activities seriously, you've learned an extensive amount about your inner thoughts, beliefs and values. That learned knowledge is power. Since you have the power of knowing a lot more about who you are and what you believe, I invite you to put that inquisitive hat on again and ask yourself several more questions.

I'm called *The Couples Cure™ Lady*. That title comes from my inquiry-style life coaching process that assists couples with finding solutions to their relationship concerns. I challenge my clients with questions about themselves and their relationships. In that same manner, I challenge you to probe further into understanding your beliefs and behaviors in your quest for knowledge. Ask yourself: What am I most pleased with about myself? Do I have any beliefs, behaviors or other personal attributes that I want to modify to make me a better person? Of course, you know that modifications mean change.

Now that you have this powerful knowledge about who you really are, the next questions follow a natural sequence. My questions to you again are three: What needs to be changed? What's your plan? When do you plan to make these changes?

Further, I would be remiss, as a life coach, if I failed to direct you to be candid with yourself — and ask several additional questions:

1. Do I honestly want the very best relationship possible?

2. Do I feel I deserve the best relationship or am I doing things to sabotage my relationships?

3. What am I doing, as an active participant, to make life with my partner better?

These questions are telling about your state of mind. They provide insight regarding your feelings about your relationship, what you want from your relationship and what you're willing to do.

Embracing Change Self Assessment

Knowing and accepting that you are exactly where you are supposed to be in your relationship based on your prior actions and environment is powerful knowledge. If you want to modify, change or enhance anything about your life and relationship, then a somber evaluation of how you manage change is in order. If you're one of those Type A personalities or genius level scholars who likes to jump ahead when reading a novel before plowing through the entire book, then this comment is for you: **Go back and review; complete the exercises in the Steps 1 - Self Knowledge and Step 2 - Mindset before you proceed.** If, on the other hand you're working this book sequentially, then read on. You know that this chapter is about understanding and accepting that change will occur in every aspect of your life.

To begin this journey of personal transformation, the first stage in the process is to take an assessment and truly evaluate your personal behavior. This assessment is designed to stimulate your thought processes. You'll be guided to think about and reflect on your skills and behavior when change occurs in your life.

This is a fun, yet revealing self-scoring activity that will allow you to gauge your ability to adjust to the changes in your life. The questions are thought-provoking and provide insight about your values, behavior and actions when it comes to managing the inevitable change in your life.

Take out a piece of paper and list the numbers 1-10 on the left hand side. Read each statement of the *Embracing Change Self Assessment* that follows and rate yourself on a scale of 1 to 3 (1 = Not Ever, 2 = Sometimes, 3 = Often). This is where your personal integrity comes into play. No one other than you will have access to your score sheet. Only you know the real answers. As you review each statement, be honest with yourself.

Embracing Change Self-Assessment

1. I establish a proactive mindset and initiate changes in my personal life.

2. I maintain an attitude that change is positive and I welcome change.

3. I look for the future benefits of change

4. I am careful to be realistic and avoid overly expectant results about change.

5. I expect some resistance, questions, and reactions to change and I prepare how best to respond.

6. My own behavior is easy going concerning the need for change.

7. I enjoy change.

8. I assess change in my life and divide it into smaller manageable pieces.

9. I look forward to, celebrate and welcome change.

10. I embrace change in my personal life.

After rating all statements, take a close look at your answers. Your responses reflect your ability, or lack thereof, to embrace change. If the majority of your responses to the first 10 statements fall into the category of "1 = not ever" or "2 = sometimes," then you know that there is work to be done. If however the majority of your scores are "3 = often," that's a good thing. Congratulations! You handle change well. Regardless of your score, it is human nature to be the best you can.

You may want to refer to the *Embracing Change Self-Assessment* as an easy reference and coaching tool to help you embrace change in your life.

Beginning your personal transformation is difficult. I understand that. Know also that my responsibility to you as a reader of this book is to help you to find clarity in your current situation. My job is to help you discover, clarify, and align with whatever goals you wish to achieve. My inquiry-based coaching process encourages self-discovery. I coach with the understanding and knowledge that you, the reader/client, possess all of the answers to your life and relationship solutions. A good coach will never tell you what the answer is. My job is to hold you accountable and responsible for your own solutions, while bringing out the best in you as your personal transformation occurs.

No doubt you have heard the concept: *Change your thoughts, change your life.* That concept is more than a notion. This principle actually works. I know from what I speak! Here are a few solutions to help pave the way to a new lifestyle and relationship.

Mastering The Art Of Change In Your Life

Discard Old Beliefs

Your thoughts and beliefs about your relationship need to be closely examined. You've taken on a new perspective about your life and relationship. Dissect every belief and aspect of your life regarding your personal activities and within your relationship. Are those old beliefs facts or are they fiction? Are they true? Or are they assumptions? If they are not absolutely true and cannot be verified as to their accuracy, then you must replace those thoughts and beliefs with new ones which allow the truth to resurface. Don't assume anything!

Don't Make Assumptions

Find the courage to ask questions and express what you really want. Communicate with others as clearly as you can to avoid misunderstandings, sadness, and drama. With just this one agreement, you can completely transform your life.

Don Miguel Ruiz,
from The Four Agreements

Feel The Fear And Do It Anyway

Feel the fear and do it anyway. You've heard that before. We are all troubled by assuming that if we make the first move, we will appear weak. We're afraid of what might occur. The typical human being, for whatever reason, sometimes assumes the worst without any justification whatsoever. Think about those challenging times that you've had in the past. Recall once when you had a situation that you were fearful of and you did it anyway. You accomplished that task and you're better off because of your actions. What a relief! As you reflect on that situation you realize and you know in your heart that what you thought to be a challenging situation was not the case at all.

Do Things Differently

Regardless of where you are in your relationship, now is the time to begin to do things differently. Whatever the approach has been to solving your relationship challenges, know that there is a different way -- very possibly a better way. Ask yourself these questions: *If not now, then when? How long do I want to continue in this kind of relationship? If it's not good, you have the power to change it. If it's good, you can always improve it.*

Make a paradigm shift to 180° of what you're currently doing. Whatever is going on in your relationship, make a commitment to do things differently.

Thoroughly examine your relationship. If it's not what you want or what you deserve, then now's the time to make that paradigm shift. If you have the kind of personality that likes to take things slowly, now's the time to move things along much more quickly. If your personality is such that you like to make sure that you have all of the facts about a circumstance or situation before you make a move, toss that plan out. In many instances you get bogged down with data -- too much detail and you become immobile. If you're prone to move slowly because you don't like to make mistakes, again toss that philosophy out and make more mistakes. It's the person who recovers from mistakes and takes those mistakes as learning opportunities, so it doesn't happen again, who really gains control of his or her life. Don't focus on the problem. Focus on the solution.

It truly takes two people to either make or break a relationship. The sooner you step up to the plate and acknowledge your part in the challenge, the easier it will be to become an active part of the solution. The key here is to acknowledge your responsibility and discontinue the finger-pointing. Be ready to be the change!

Imagine A New You And Your New Life

Imagine a new you. Who are you as this new person? What would you like to be? How would you like to behave? What do you want to change about yourself? Imagine a new you and all of the positive attributes, characteristics and personality traits that you want and deserve. Then, imagine the kind of relationship you want with your partner or significant other. Make a list. Close your eyes. See it. Believe it. Know it. **Now do it and make it happen.**

Now that you're armed with working knowledge about how you manage your own personal change in your life, what do you plan to do about it? Again, ask yourself the following questions:

- What do I need to do?

- What do I need to do to change?

- What is required of me to not only manage change, but also embrace change?

- How can I anticipate change to better improve myself and enhance my relationship?

The last step of *The Couples Cure™ Book, Mastering the Art of Relationships in 7 Easy Steps* is **Take Action Now**. This is a step-by-step process, designed to guide you through creating an easy to use *Action Plan*. This action plan will help you implement a simple, workable change strategy that you can use right now to begin to get the relationship and life you deserve. The simple plan will highlight the skills and the basic tools to help you deal with change management. That's what embracing change and welcoming change into your life is called — Change Management! You can't stop change. You also know that change is inevitable. And yet, even though you are an intelligent, practical human being, change is difficult for you and a lot of people. You're not alone. However, new strategies and behavior will help ease the process of learning to embrace change in your relationship. You'll be equipped to more easily manage all the changes in your life.

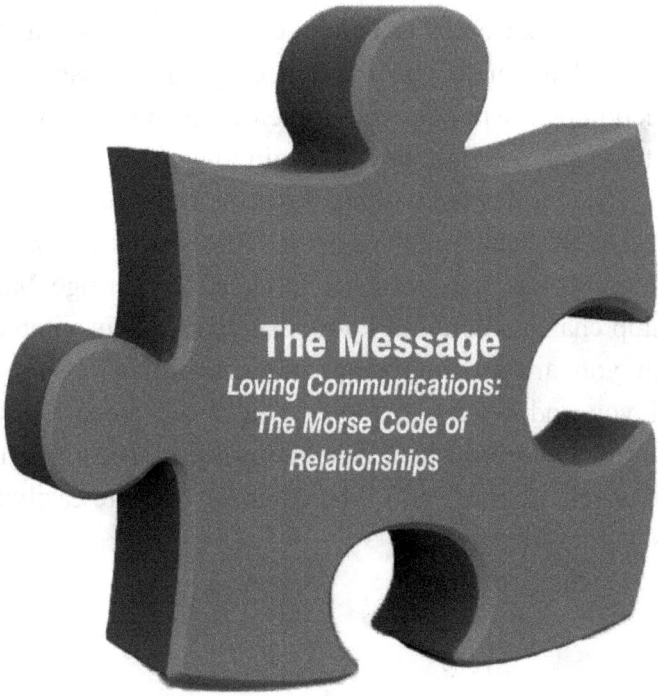

The Message
Loving Communications:
The Morse Code of
Relationships

Chapter 4: The Message

Loving Communications:
The Morse Code Of Relationships

*The quality of our life is based
on the quality of our communication with ourselves
and with the outside world.*

Milton H. Erickson

Communication Is The Key

Step 4 in *The Couples Cure™ Book, Mastering the Art of Relationships in 7 Easy Steps* is **The Message, Loving Communications: The Morse Code of Relationships.** Communications in the context of this chapter addresses the how and way you relate to, express your interpersonal thoughts and feelings and connect with your partner. The subtitle of this chapter, The Morse Code of Relationships, conveys the essence of relationship communications.

Aside from this book, Morse Code is a method of sending electronic signals and messages using the alphabet or code in which the letters are represented by a combination of long and short signals of light or sound. The Morse Code is a communication method typically used in industrial, military and business applications. Technicians who utilize the code undergo extensive training and study to master the Morse Code transmission and reception technology to enable them to communicate effectively. This effectiveness requires employing signal representation, timing and intention. The Morse Code is a uniquely different language. It is complex to those of us who are not familiar with the intricate and delicate syntax. Unless you are knowledgeable and familiar with Morse Code transmissions and signaling, communications would be improbable if not impossible.

Unfortunately, individuals rarely, if ever take courses or get training on how to communicate with their partner, regardless of the language. In my conversations with hundreds of people who expressed their relationship experiences, the vast majority complained that communications issues with their partners was a source of conflict and quite the force to be reckoned with. Hence, the subtitle: **The Morse Code of Relationships**.

My experience with many couples revealed that their communication skills are shallow and suffer from the inability to effectively communicate. Men, women, young, old, long term partnerships, married, and all along the continuum of relationships said that at one time or another -- or worse yet, fairly often -- their partner just didn't know how to communicate with them. Although they used different terms to express their frustration, what they believed and said is that they (both partners) lacked the skills and the ability to convey and receive the message. It was as though they were speaking two different languages. They went on to say that both partners were deficient and lacked the know-how to deliver and receive the message. They simply couldn't represent, time and deliver the intended message with precision. Hence, the Morse Code effect. Their exchanges were either misunderstood or not understood at all.

The communication factor alone can make or break your relationship. One of the most essential steps in mastering the art of relationships is your ability to master the couples' Morse Code and successfully deliver and receive your intended message. To put it bluntly, your ability to effectively communicate with your partner is vital to mastering the art of your relationship at any stage, at any time. It's a simple matter of the way you communicate with your partner.

The number of broken relationships and the increase in the number of divorces have reached epidemic proportions. Divorces and partnership dissolutions are in a state of crisis in America. Currently, the divorce rate in the U.S. is at an all time high of 50+% for first time marriages.

Singles and couples alike are beginning to take notice and discuss how best to improve and enhance relationships. Couples are seeking relationship coaches to learn how to stabilize their domestic partnerships. Once they understand the fundamental role that communications has in partnerships, couples eagerly express interest in changing their behavior. They want to preserve or improve what they currently have. Partners want to avoid becoming another separated couple or divorce statistic.

Clearly, remedies that formerly worked to preserve intimate partnerships are no longer effective. What were considered successful nineteenth and twentieth century relationship cures, just don't work anymore. The commitment level of couples to work on their relationship has declined. The plain, sad truth is that men and women are afraid to invest energy and effort into preserving what they have. You make excuses: *"Well, if I open up and let her know how vulnerable I am and how much I really want to save this relationship, I may get hurt."* Worse yet, you say: *"She may not feel the same way; she may not want to save our relationship and will reject me."* And so, you do nothing. The condition of your relationship gets worse. And what was once your fun-loving, intimate partnership takes on the form and experiences of the infamous relationship roller coaster ride. If you've been through any kind of break-up before or known couples who have, you know exactly what I'm referring to. I call that stage of relationships the declining rollercoaster ride. The declining ride progression starts at the top of the roller coaster and has a series of ups and downs. The ups never get as high as the top of the roller coaster (or the beginning of the relationship). The relationship continues in a steady downward motion until months, years, and decades of decline ultimately result in a flat line where both partners are terribly unhappy. Sometimes the effects culminate in partners having contempt for each other.

The decline and the eventual erosion of feelings are typically the result of one primary issue — communication or lack thereof!

Communication issues and money-related problems are the number one and number two reasons couples get divorced in the United States. Depending on the study, some researchers list money as number one, while others show communication problems as the reigning cause for separations and ultimate divorce for married couples in the U.S. Not sex. Not adultery. Not physical abuse or mental cruelty. Yes, communication! Notwithstanding the significant role money-related issues have on relationships, communication and/or the lack thereof is quite often the real underlying basis for failed marriages, broken relationships, and unhappy partnerships in the United States.

Poor Communication = Irreconcilable Differences

In divorce courts, two other terms used to describe a couple's relationship woes regarding communications are irreconcilable differences and incompatibility. These two definitions are also used to explain misunderstandings, misinterpretations, and your inability to hold a respectful discussion with your partner. Frankly, it doesn't matter whether the justification is lack of communication, poor communication skills, irreconcilable differences, or incompatibility, the net effect is your inability to communicate with your partner and/or your partner's inability to communicate with you.

Irreconcilable differences, incapability, and communication challenges were the same findings I confirmed during my personal discussions, interviews and surveys with individuals, married couples, and divorcees who experienced failed relationships. The number one issue in their opinion was the inability of the two partners to discuss in a civilized manner the little things in life. Those little things turned into bigger things...with frustration. The bigger things with frustration continued to grow into anger. And, the anger resulted in one or both partners initiating an argument. Frequent arguments ultimately trigger the beginning of the end of a relationship. Then two things happen: first, the couple is unable to discuss not only the subject of the argument, and second, the couple becomes incapable of discussing almost anything.

It is difficult to quantify how significant communications, or lack thereof, is a factor in the breakup of partners that were not married. What we know for sure is that irreconcilable differences and communication are the number one reason for documented divorce in the United States. This show-stopping home wrecker can be attributed to married couples as well as any other committed relationship or partnership. Irreconcilable differences relate to incompatibility, conflicts, opposing/disagreeing positions when two people are unable to come to an agreeable solution. The key factor in all the aforementioned reasons for irreconcilable differences can be summed up in one word: communications!

Your ability to communicate with your partner and yourself (your internal mindset and your mental attitude) about your relationship are two elements of communication that determine whether or not your relationship will survive. In addition to communications, your mindset will be the other determining factor as to whether or not your relationship weathers the typical partnership storms. When your mindset is not one of commitment, surely you can and will be counted as a statistic in the divorce rates quoted above or in broken relationships.

What I know with certainty is that the essence of your communication is what makes or breaks your relationships. This chapter will challenge you to think about your own mindset and communication skills. I invite you to examine your behavior when it comes to communicating with your partner, mate, lover, or spouse.

You'll have an opportunity to review effective communications skills and compare your own abilities in the areas of proactive listening, problem solving, communication sensitivities, and how you deal with interpersonal conflict. In addition, you'll get key communication tools to help you negotiate a resolution when difficulties and challenges arise in your life.

Communication Challenges: Signs Of Problems

Quite often, what appears to be the obvious problem, poor communication, may not be the problem at all. The use of the expression "poor communications" is frequently identified as a catch-all phrase or unknowingly used for convenience to put any number of other issues in a basket. It is merely indicative of some deeper core issues that affect relationships. For example, if there is a lack of trust, respect, or honesty in the relationship, the chances are that any discussion between partners will be tainted and most likely result in contempt for one another or no communications at all. Why? The reason is that trust, respect, and honesty are all values. The significance of values is well defined in the chapter on Self Knowledge. If you've not already done so, read the chapter on values first; then return here to continue with *The Couples Cure™ System*.

Regardless of how you answered the questions about your values, all is not lost. Keep reading. Have you read Napoleon Hill's *Think and Grow Rich* or T. Harv Eker's *Secrets of the Millionaire Mind: Mastering the Inner Game of Wealth*? The title of these best sellers may be misleading. No doubt they address money, how to get it, and how to keep it. But the real messages presented in these treasures are the golden nuggets that speak to your values and mindset. It's the gems throughout these books that cause you to think about how your own mind and attitude work. Although these best sellers are about money (which will be addressed later in this book), these books also begin to lay the foundation for a total transformation of your attitude. These authors create an environment that begins to change the way you think about things.

So, what is your attitude and mindset about your relationship? What's your attitude about repairing your personal relationship with your significant other? Have you thought about working on your communication skills to improve your relationship with your partner?

Go ahead, admit it. The excuses you make are all fear based. The tendency is to mask your real feelings. Cover those feelings up with some less dramatic sounding words such as "apprehensive," "scared," "concerned," and "frightened." These are cowardly words you use to hide your true colors. There is fear in your heart — whether it's minor or major — you're afraid of having your feelings and your heart hurt. The operative word here is FEAR. It's an old cliché. Recall that the contemporary definition of fear is: **F**alse **E**vidence **A**ppearing **R**eal. FEAR is the number one culprit responsible for killing the initiative in maintaining and enhancing relationships. Fear and the perceived inability of human beings to overcome their emotional crutch is what prevents people from being happy. Fear prevents people from pursuing their dreams because they're afraid they might fail. For the reasons stated above, when it comes to fear, you do nothing or very little to improve your relationship thereby allowing the downward decline in your relationship to continue.

> *The relationship is*
> *the communication bridge between people.*
>
> Alfred Kadushin

What we've got here is failure to communicate. The grimaced-faced, exasperated Guard Captain loathingly addressed the Florida prisoner, Paul Newman's character -- Cool Hand Luke, in the 1967 blockbuster movie by the same name. This Best Actor nominee's character refused to surrender to the prison system. As a result of Cool Hand Luke's obstinate behavior, the frustrated Captain described the aggravated relationship between himself and Luke as a failure to communicate. These three words, failure to communicate, fittingly illustrate the age old condition when two people in a relationship misunderstand, misinterpret, or simply don't get it; or they are unwilling to compromise, as in the case of Paul Newman's character in the movie.

The Message Solutions

There are two schools of thought when debating solutions to couples' Morse Code relationship challenges with delivering and receiving the message. The debate concerns the very nature of the process of communication. Is the process of communication an art or is it a science?

The first school of thought subscribes to the notion that effective communication is an art because of the fluidity of the human emotions engaged during the communication process. Meaning, that communication is generally loose with no real defined structure when you talk to your intimate partner. This school of thought addresses the ease with which partners engage, much like sitting on a sun-kissed beach watching the ebb and flow of seamless waves on a summer's eve in the aqua waters of the Caribbean Ocean.

The second school of thought claims that communication is a science. This thought suggests that there are specific scientific rules that are applicable during the communication processes.

It doesn't matter whether you feel communication is an art or a science. The real question to ask yourself is: How can you ensure you are an effective communicator - particularly in your most intimate relationships?

The following pages contain questions and exercises that will stimulate your thought process and cause you to think about your ability to communicate. I'll help you take a close look at your own communication techniques and interpersonal competencies when it comes to dealing with other people, especially in you personal relationships. You'll also assess your proactive listening skills and your problem solving ability. Why, you might ask, are proactive listening and problem solving addressed in this chapter on communication? The answer is simple. Good communications require as much (if not more) active listening as it does speaking.

Next, you'll be challenged to put yourself under your honest microscope and answer this question: How do you know when you are communicating effectively?

Communication Defined

Webster defines communication as: *"a means or method... In the process of dealing with others, communication is the way we transfer and exchange our ideas and perceptions...* Traditionally, good communication is conveying a message so that the sender and receiver attain mutual understanding."

Senders And Receivers Of Messages

In its simplest form, any attempt to communicate requires two components: a sender and a receiver. It takes two to communicate. Understand that in this chapter I address communication between two people, which includes the spoken and unspoken messages expressed between two partners. The Morse Code methodology of communicating requires the presence of an encoder and a decoder to affect human communications. When communications are good between two human beings, the message is received exactly as the sender intended. The channel is clear. There is no room for interpretation, or misunderstandings.

Take the case of a new born baby. The baby is unable to talk, yet the mother clearly understands what the baby needs. The mother understands when the baby needs food, a change of diaper, is sleepy or simply irritable. A perceptive mother who is in sync with her infant senses what the baby needs by the sound of her cry. Now this sensitivity may take a few hours, days, or weeks to develop; however before long the mother intuitively knows what the new born wants as soon as the baby girl begins that first sign of whimpering. In spite of the newness of the infant, she is an excellent communicator. And the mother strives to be the best, most responsive parent possible; the mother is totally receptive to the baby's communication methods.

Think about the relationships between a parent and a toddler in his second year, often referred to as the terrible-two phase. (Personally I like to refer to them as the terrific two's because this is the stage when toddlers begin to explore their surroundings and flex their newly found life skills and communication muscles.) I can't tell you how many parents told me that they were at their wits end dealing with little Johnnie during this period. I usually laughed and reminded them that Johnnie is a very effective communicator. He is the sender, and the parent is the receiver. If Johnnie didn't get exactly what he wanted, his usual response was to fall on the floor, legs and arms flailing in every direction until he got his way or whatever he wanted. In my opinion, that is very effective communication. The sender, Johnnie, communicated his unhappiness in the form of exaggerated body language; and the receiver, his parent, was the recipient of his communicative expressions and thoroughly understood Johnnie's needs. The parent got it. By the way, Johnnie was usually very observant and realized that this form of expressive body language got him what he wanted. That is, until Mom or Dad helped Johnnie modify his behavior or gently coerced him in to changing his outbursts in lieu of spankings.

How good are you at transferring and exchanging ideas, and sending messages to your receiver? By the end of this chapter, you'll find out how you interact with your partner. You'll have an opportunity to examine your own communication behavior and you'll receive several golden nuggets and easy tools to help you improve your communication skills right now.

Men & Women Are Different...Thank Goodness!

Yes! Women and men are supposed to be different! Thank goodness for the difference. How boring life would be if we were all the same. It's the diversity in life that adds spice to relationships.

Men and women differ in both communication style and emotional needs. The uniqueness of men and women can be chalked up to the "wiring" of the respective genders. Or as my recently deceased Uncle Wendell Flagg would say, *"It's in their DNA and they simply can't help themselves."* It is these very same differences along with the openness to love, that cause us to adore one another and yet, experience the deepest and most painful emotional heartache and heartbreak.

Dr. John Gray's *Men Are From Mars, Women Are From Venus* clearly delineates the differences and some of the similarities between men and women. In his best seller, Dr. Gray takes inventory of the key emotional and communicative dynamics between men and women, including behavioral differences. He also points out the differences in problem solving where men typically prefer to work independently to resolve an issue; and women typically become more communicative in developing resolutions to issues. Differences in communication styles are also addressed. Dr. Gray suggests that men like to get to the point compared to women who sometimes like to engage in talking and are happy to listen. He also addresses what is often referred to as the basic survival instinct. A man's instinct is to look after himself and his family, while a woman's tendency is to be a nurturer and look out for others. In talking to one another, he says that men tend to talk for the purpose of relaying information and women tend to talk to fully express their feelings.

Dr. Gray also highlights the need for valuing one another's differences in expectations, giving, and the essentials of dealing with unresolved negative feelings.

Communication Indicates Where You Are In Life

"The quality of our lives is based on our ability to communicate with the outside world and ourselves..." These few words by Milton H. Erikson are some of the most significant words in this chapter. Take a minute to ponder his statement. The reason his words are so powerful is because he says where you are in life is directly related to your ability to communicate.

Your ability to communicate effectively is one of the most critical life skills you can cultivate as a human being. Your communication skills affect every aspect of your life. The ability to attain mutual understanding through effective communication affects your work and professional relationships, marriages, partnerships, personal associations and business partnerships. Conversely, poor communications frequently cause conflicts, hurt feelings, create confusion, and no doubt contribute to broken relationships.

The Clairvoyant Effect

I've often said jokingly, in a tenuous situation: *"I'm good, but I'm not clairvoyant. I'm good, but I'm not clairvoyant translates to – I really do understand the English language quite well; unfortunately, I'm not a mind reader."*

Say What You Mean—A Lesson For Women

Women have been accused of expecting their partners to understand what they're feeling, even though they may not say specifically what's on their mind. If you are a woman, use this time to take a personal assessment of how you communicate. Sisters, let us begin now to pay special attention to how we convey our thoughts. I've heard time and time again from men that women don't necessarily convey feelings and thoughts with preciseness. I've had conversations with both men and women about the topic of conversing in intimate relationships as well as professional and business relationships and the comments are typically the same: *"Women can be vague when it comes to addressing issues head-on and dealing with what might be considered an unpleasant situation."*

Long gone are the days when it was considered feminine to be coy, to speak delicately and not express your honest and open feelings. If you're one of those women, forget that archaic behavior. It may have worked at some point in history, but now is not the time to pretend to be delicate and coy. Now more than ever, women and men alike must stand tall and be counted on to deliver the message as it is intended to be received.

My Word Is Law—A Lesson For Men

I've also heard repeatedly from women: *"Men tend to fly off the handle during difficult intimate conversations and then withdraw without expressing their feelings or explaining the reasons for their outburst."* Below is one such example.

Christine and Max, both in their mid-forties, have been married for 15 years. To most everyone, other than Christine and Max, they were considered to have a great marriage. According to Christine and Max, their marriage wasn't bad. It wasn't great. It was ok. They never openly talked about the status of their marriage with any of their friends or family.

One day, Christine decided to confide in me. She said, *"I've come to you because I'm exasperated. I want more from my marriage."* *"How so?"* I asked. *"What do you have now? And what do you mean when you say you want more?"* *"Well..."* she said, *"I want more. I want a more exciting intimate relationship with my husband. What I have now is the Saturday night special."*

"What's the Saturday night special?" I asked. *"You know, we get intimate every Saturday night and it's the same-old, same-old. It's gotten to a point where it is obligatory sex. It's missionary position sex. It's the same thing we've been doing*

for the past 15 years. I want more! I want to feel special. I want to engage in a fair amount of foreplay. I want to feel like I'm desired. I need to feel wanted. I want the intimacy."

She continued, *"Right now I feel like I want to scream every time I think about our Saturday night special. I am just so frustrated. It's gotten to a point where he thinks I don't enjoy sex at all. He thinks I don't want to have sex. Since he thinks I don't enjoy or want to have sex. Our Saturday night specials become fewer and farther between."*

"Have you talked with Max about your thoughts?" "Does he know how you feel?" "Yes", she said. *"I've talked with him a number of times. It's very difficult to talk with him about intimate subjects. It's infuriating to talk about sex with him; especially when it's about wanting more. He feels as though I'm attacking his manhood. That's not it. I only want to improve the quality and intimacy of our sex life. We tried dozens of times.*

He only gets mad; he gets defensive; he gets loud. He keeps saying, 'I'm doing what you've asked for. I tried it that way and you didn't like it.' He thinks that what he's doing is right and is good." *"Well is it?"* I asked. *"Not only is it not good,"* Christine complained, *"his actions have become a turn-off!"*

"Now, every time we talk about improving our intimate times together, Max blows up, he yells, he yells loudly. He seems to think that the louder he shouts, the more he proves that his point of view is right. He acts as if his word is the law and that no other option or opinion is to be considered. He's often been known to say: 'I can't talk to you at all; we've got a serious communication problem.' He just stops talking and storms out of the room. Then he gives me the cold shoulder and we don't talk for days, sometime weeks."

Men, let this be a lesson to you. Go back several pages and re-read the section with the title: **Communication Challenges: Symptoms of Other Problems.** Christine and Max don't have a communication problem. Their problem is intimacy. Max's issue is that he becomes defensive. He chooses not to address the situation. He then takes the position that his word is law.

Gentlemen, when your partner wants to talk about your intimate relationship, take her at face value. She means no harm. It's highly unlikely she wants to destroy you or insult your manhood. Do your very best even though you've tried before. This is the time to try again. Try something different. Be willing to work with you partner. The probability is that she wants to truly improve the situation. Work with her. Of all the sensitive conversations, your intimate conversations are the most challenging. When you get the chapter on **Platinum Sex Rule**, spend time digesting the fun techniques about win-win sex for you and your partner. You'll no longer take the position that your word is the law. That chapter will also improve your communication skills. Trust me, you'll be much better off as a result.

Think about some of your own situations. You can relate to intimate challenges in your own life, family and partnerships where there were major communication breakdowns of what appeared to be minor issues that could be resolved with good communication skills. Yet, when these conditions occur, partners and family members don't talk for days, weeks, sometimes months and years.

The Real Deal About Communications

Communications is a substantial part of who we are as human beings. Numerous studies reflect that human communication is comprised of two components: verbal communication and non verbal communication. It is estimated that our verbal, or actual words, comprise only 7% of our communication effort; while the non-verbal consists of the remaining 93%, including a combination of 38% of the tone of voice and 55% body language. With such a large percentage of our communication skills residing in the realm of non-verbal communications, it's no wonder that the communication challenge lies square on the shoulders of the decoder. The decoder or receiver in the two person communication mode is responsible for deciphering 93% of everything that is said.

There are various non-verbal forms of communication. Much more communication is expressed and conveyed in your physical appearance that you realize. Your posture, facial expressions, gestures, and the tone of your voice all convey different things about you.

- When you are engaged in a conversation with your partner, what does your posture say about you?

- Are you attentive?

- Do you reflect the posture of someone who is truly interested in what your partner is saying?

- Are you in the moment?

- Do you hold on to every word expressed by your partner or are you distracted?

- Are your thoughts elsewhere? Are you thinking about things that happened earlier in the day or something that caught your attention yesterday?

If you think your partner isn't aware that you are disingenuous, think again! Our physical body movements, facial expressions, and gestures are all dead giveaways to our partners and clearly indicate when we are not in the moment, listening to our partner. And they know it! You may think you're subtle and pretend to give your partner your undivided attention. Well, you can forget about it! Whoever you are talking with knows instantly that your mind is elsewhere.

Do you show your partner that you are interested when he/she is talking to you? Are you multi-tasking while they're spilling their gut to you about how delightful or terrible their day at the office was? Are you checking email when you're talking with your mate who may be going through the crisis of their lifetime? Do you give your partner your undivided attention without being asked?

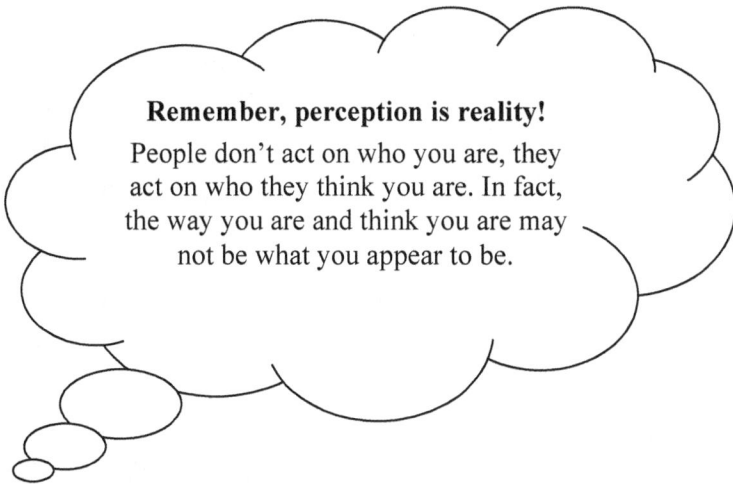

Remember, perception is reality!
People don't act on who you are, they act on who they think you are. In fact, the way you are and think you are may not be what you appear to be.

What Message Do You Project?

Have you ever had someone misinterpret what you say? Do you feel people sometimes misunderstand the intent of what you wanted to convey? Or, has anyone told you that your personality is 180 degrees different than what your external image projects? Do you recall a time when someone said they didn't like you even without knowing you or anything about you? Or worse yet, have people ever said, *Wow! You don't appear to be that kind of person.*

The Past Determines The Present

The real communication challenge is that everyone hears and perceives differently — all interpretations are based on your past experiences and perceptions. Perception is reality. Remember, people don't act on who you are. They act on who THEY THINK you are. In fact, the way you are may not be what you appear to be. Your own assessment of who you are and the type of personality, characteristics, qualities, and personal traits you think you possess and project are quite often considerably different than what others perceive you to be. Chances are you appear to be different to other people than the image you have of yourself.

One might ask, why is that so? Why is there disparity between what is real and what is perceived? The simple answer is that perception is a process. Perception is the process of using the senses to acquire information about the surrounding environment, situation, or person. Human senses are based on our past experiences. We all have different frames of reference which are created in a 'building block' or stacking manner. Our experiential radar scope results from a number of factors such as our experiences, personal history, childhood education, familial upbringing and the socio-economic and educational environment in which we lived and were raised.

Instant Assessment

Years ago before I was married, it was not uncommon for me to say that I could successfully assess the longevity of my relationship with any potential suitor by the way he greeted me. I would make the assessment within the first thirty seconds of our meeting. And, with a very slim margin of error, I could accurately predict how far our relationship was going by the way the person communicated with me. I could also tell if there would be a date or not. I could also immediately tell if there was a possibility of a long-term relationship and if there was potential of "going together".

How is that possible you may ask? How can you predict how long a relationship you'll have with that person in less than one hour? The response is simple—our relationships are based on our level of communication. Our intimate associations, personal contacts, business relations and personal affairs are all predicated on how we communicate and the quality of our verbal and physical exchanges.

Right or wrong, that first impression is everlasting. Sometimes your first impression can be changed over time; however most of the time what you think of a person from the moment you meet him or her is the lasting impression.

External Assessment

In my *Effective Communication* workshops, The Askia Group students are given the opportunity to participate in and receive an external image assessment from people they don't know. The exercise provides the individual with instant feedback on what kind of image they project. The assessment is based on their appearance and verbal communications. My students are always fascinated by their results. Invariably, most of my students will say, *"I didn't realize I projected that kind of image."* or *"That's not at all what or who I am."* This exercise is essential because the external image assessment is accomplished by and with people who don't know you and have never met you. Therefore their opinions and responses are likely to be far more objective. As a matter of fact, one of the ground rules for the activity is to be honest, yet fair and compassionate in sharing thoughts and opinions. Some of the questions from our *External Image Assessment* include: What do you think this person does for a living? What is the first (overall) impression they convey to you? Each person rates the image they are projecting using a scale from 1-10 where 1 = poor or lowest level, and 10 = great or the highest level. What kind of image do you project?

Your Response Makes The Difference

> *It's not what is said or what happens,*
> *rather it is how you respond to what is said or*
> *what happens that makes the difference*
> *in the quality of your relationships...*
>
> Reverend Doctor Eloise Oliver

One of my favorite teacher-ministers, Reverend Doctor Eloise Oliver, frequently says during her Sunday morning message, "*It's not what is said or what happens, rather how you respond to what is said or what happens that makes the big difference in the quality of your relationships.*" Silence is golden! It makes a most interesting response to anyone who tries to provoke you into a conversation about something you've decided not to participate in. After all, it takes two people to argue or two people to start a fight. If one or the other chooses to take the high road, the other partner can't pick a fight. What happens in your relationship is all about choice. Just try choosing to take the high road and see what happens. When your hot buttons have been pushed by your partner, or you're about to be provoked into a heated discussion, take the high road. Taking the high road means that, if you're provoked, your choice is to remain calm. You will not engage in a heated debate, regardless of your habit and pattern of defending your position. In this instance, choose to not engage. Instead opt to say, "*This is not the place nor time to discuss this. I don't necessarily agree, and I'm not going to argue with you.*" Then, sit back and watch what happens.

Even if you choose to engage in a discussion or heated argument, there are certain rules of engagement that must be followed to protect the sanctity of the relationship. Relationships are volatile in the midst of a heated argument.

The Rules & Rituals Of Your Arguments Matter

Arguments: The real test of partnership stability.
How you argue makes a difference and determines a
lot about your relationship....

Prestell Askia

Early in my marriage to Kemal, it became necessary to define the parameters of our arguments. My husband and I had to sit down and literally discuss what we could do and say and could not do or say during our heated discussions. Fortunately, for the most part we had civilized arguments. Never once did we engage in any name calling. It goes without discussion when I tell you that abusive behavior was not on either mine or my husband's radar. We both agreed that kind of conduct was out of the question.

Numerous couples have used this same process to protect their relationship. The reason it was necessary to create boundaries was to ensure we preserved our relationship so we wouldn't "chip away" or "whittle away" at our parnership—ultimately destroying it to a point where there was nothing left. We needed to establish ground rules for the sake of preserving our relationship. We went to a local restaurant, sat down at a quiet table in the corner with a glass of red wine and developed *The Couples Code of Honor*. (An expanded explanation of this agreement and parameters are highlighted in **The Argument Resolution** Section below. A free, downloadable PDF copy of *The Couples Code of Honor* template is also available at TheCouplesCureBook.com.) Little did I know at that time that this was the beginning of establishing our core value system for our relationship. This was the holy grail of protecting and solidifying our precious partnership.

The following tragic illustration is a classic case of what not to do in a relationship.

I was on a Delta Flight from Washington D.C. to San Francisco. I brought up the topic of relationships with the delightful lady sitting in the seat next to me. When I asked her opinion about the three elements that make for a healthy, fulfilling relationship, the subject of communications surfaced. After several minutes of discussing her top three elements that make a healthy and fulfilling relationship, I paused as I asked, *"Norma, why was the art and science of communications so important to you and your former marriage?"*

As she shook her head she said: *"Note the use of former marriage, Had my husband and I really understood the fine art and delicate science of effective communications between two people in a committed relationship, we'd probably still be together now. That was the primary thing that destroyed our relationship. It also destroyed our respect for one another."*

As she looked at me, her eyes welled with tears. She became very emotional. I could feel the pain in her heart as she said, *"My husband and I chipped away at the one thing we had and shared together—we chipped away at our bond until there was nothing left."*

"What do you mean?" I interrupted. *"Ordinarily, I don't stop my interviews mid-sentence, but I can clearly see you're upset. Would you like some water? Or a tissue?"*

"No, I'll be fine. As I look back and analyze my marriage and the reasons for its demise, I realize that hindsight is twenty-twenty. I can see clearly now. Long ago I acknowledged that the real cause of our failed marriage was chipping."

"Chipping?" I asked as I tilted my head with a curious look on my face. *"What exactly is chipping? And how and why did chipping play such a significant role in your marriage?"*

She paused, and painstakingly said, *"Chipping is the process of whittling away, cutting out little chips of your marriage— like an artist who chips away at a piece of wood until she creates a fine artifact or carved statue. Actually it's the process of cutting away at the very fabric of your relationship and whittling down to the delicate fibers that hold the relationship together until there is literally nothing left."*

"Can you give me examples of chipping?" *"Oh yes,"* she confessed, *"I can share plenty about chipping. Seems every time my husband and I would get into arguments, we would not only quarrel about the issue at hand, we'd also complain about things that had absolutely nothing to do with the immediate subject. Invariably, those arguments were the beginning of the end of our marriage."* I continued, *"How does chipping relate to the end of your marriage? Are you suggesting that 'chipping' was the one thing that was a deal breaker and, if eliminated, could have saved your marriage?"* Norma responded, *"Yes! That was the one thing I would have changed! The way we quarreled, name calling, and showing little respect for one another was the catalyst that whittled away at our marriage one argument at a time."*

We all know many couples that fight and bicker constantly. In the midst of heated arguments, these couples quite often use sarcasm to attack one another. Rather than addressing whatever the subject is, they attack one another personally. These couples say hurtful things in an attempt to win an argument. They call one another foul names and engage in personal verbal attacks. These are relationships where there are no established rules about how to argue. There are no codes or guidelines that provide for respectful relations when you argue or how to handle a simple disagreement.

It has also been my experience that some people are just interested in winning an argument or being right about something. In these cases, one of the partners will do most anything to come out victorious in a disagreement. Some of their tactics include attacking their partner's character and calling them repulsive names, sometimes to a point of no repair. It doesn't matter what the circumstances are, nor is there an effort to resolve the situation; the entire effort is to win the argument. In this scenario you loose. You see, in this **win at any cost method** of solving issues in your relationship, you lose not only the battle, but you lose the entire war.

Watch Your Thoughts, Words And Actions

Extensive research by psychologists and marriage counselors reveals that there are several key ingredients that help couples weather the storm when it comes to arguments. Let's be realistic. No partnership is perfect. There will be disagreements. Many times the disagreements will be small; sometimes huge. On occasion, there may be arguments that fall into the category of downright dirty fights, You know the type I'm referring to: those where in a heated argument the personalities turn into near-monsters and the vocal outbursts progressively rise to decibel levels that would break a Memorex glass. This progressively negative behavior is the reason each relationship needs pre-determined rules for argument.

> *Watch your thoughts; they become words.*
> *Watch your words; they become actions.*
> *Watch your actions; they become habits.*
> *Watch your habits; they become character.*
> *Watch your character; it becomes your destiny.*
>
> Author Unknown
> Source: Communication Motivation Quotes

You may think that it sounds ridiculous to set "rules" and parameters for arguing, but consider the following rules the key to saving a partnership or marriage. The reason rules and parameters are set for arguments, heated discussions, and disagreements is to preserve the partnership. Consider the need for both you and your partner to be civilized in your discussions. Far too often arguments bring about the worst in you. Arguments can sometimes be a catalyst for you and your partner to let loose of emotions, behavior, and verbal attacks that you would never engage in under any other circumstance.

A healthy relationship cannot work between two people if they are unable to communicate and conduct themselves in a civilized manner. Interestingly, arguments bring out the worst in us, and in heated arguments some of the things we say can sometimes do irreparable harm to the relationship.

The Argument Resolution

The key is to discuss and agree upon these rules with your partner early in your relationship — when you're not fighting and long before you ever have an argument. You and your partner must agree to stick to these rules. By all means, when you are engaged in a quarrel or disagreement, try not to deviate from your rules. Partnership involves commitment and part of that commitment includes working together.

Regardless of where you are in your relationship, you and your partner can work together to create your own rules. I've developed a form to help you get started. You and your partner can use *The Couples Code of Honor* to create your personal rules for argument. Each partnership is unique and has different requirements. The key is to stick to the rules.

The Couples Code of Honor
Our Agreement & Parameters for Arguments

A free, downloadable copy of *The Couples Code of Honor* is available at TheCouplesCureBook.com. The PDF template provides a simple format for committed couples to create their own personalized parameters and guidelines for arguments *before* they argue.

Sticking with the guidelines and rules may not come easily at first, and you may slip up from time to time. The key is to recognize when you've broken the rules. When you or your partner break the rules, which you will inevitably do sometimes as none of us is perfect, be prepared to take swift action. This is the time to shift the old mindset paradigm. A heated argument is the time to resume control as the architect of your relationship. Change the paradigm to a new norm when you and your partner argue.

When your partner initiates a breakdown or departure from the rules, it's your responsibility to immediately address the departure. Acknowledge that you're both well intentioned and that you both signed *The Couples Code of Honor*. Remind your partner that you both must stop the argument! Immediately!

It's tough. I realize that. However, if you and your partner are serious about improving your relationship especially in the midst of a heated argument, you have to take the initiative. Stop the argument! Stop the tit-for-tat retaliatory responses. This is the time for you and your partner to say, *"Please forgive me."* or *"I forgive you...we've broken the rules of our Couples Code of Honor."* These words: *"Please forgive me"* and *"I forgive you"* allow the fiery disagreement to return to a reasonable state of normalcy; thereby permitting a civilized discussion, and hopefully, resolution of the issue. Try it. See the response from your partner. A heated discussion between you and your partner is the perfect opportunity for **you to be the change you want to see**.

You and your partner may need to revisit *The Couples Code of Honor* and your rules now and again throughout your relationship. A periodic revisit is necessarey if you and your partner find yourselves forgetting and going back to your old ways. Sometimes the guidelines may need revision. That's ok. A partnership or marriage isn't easy, but it's worth the effort.

Decoding Your Messaging Behaviors

Listed below are 24 thought-provoking questions. Be honest with yourself and avoid intentional self-deception as you ask yourself about your ability to communicate, deliver and receive the message and how you deal with disagreements in your relationship.

How Do I Communicate With My Partner?

- Do I talk loudly or yell to convince my partner that I'm right?

- Do I avoid my partner?

- Do I try to understand my partner's point of view?

- Do I fight physically or verbally?

- Do I threaten my partner? Or hold my partner hostage?

- Do I try to turn the conflict into a joke?

- Do I attempt to narrow the conflict to a specific point of agreement?

- Do I attempt to find a solution or reach a compromise?

- Do I make accusations?

- Do I view the conflict as a communication breakdown?

- Do I admit I was wrong even if I don't believe it?

- Do I exaggerate?

- Do I give in to avoid hard feelings?

- Do I concentrate on the issue rather than the person?

- Do I see the conflict as a problem solving opportunity?

- Do I yell at my partner?

- Do I refuse to listen? I know I'm right.

- Do I pretend to agree?

- Do I get another person to decide who is right?

- Do I respect my partner's opinions even if they're different from mine?

- Do I manipulate with guilt?

- Do I simply state my feelings directly and honestly?

- Do I apologize for having a different opinion?

- Do I use sarcasm?

Now that you've asked yourself the questions about how you argue with your partner, take a moment to reflect. For each question where you hesitated, answered possibly or sometimes, make the commitment to change your behavior. Do it now!

Take each of those questions and reverse your tendencies by shifting your behavior paradigm to a positive approach. Commit to amicably resolve disagreements with your partner using your new found constructive approach to disagreements.

Tactics For Communications In Difficult Situations

Wynona Judd and her mother, Naomi Judd, appeared on The Oprah Show on September 14, 2010. They discussed at length the interpersonal relationship difficulties and issues they've had for years. Naomi and Wynona also shared some of the adult communication techniques they currently use to keep their relationship on track.

The following six gems are effective for all interpersonal relationships and partnerships, in addition to the Mother-Daughter difficulties shared by the Judds. Following are phrases from that show that you can place in your communication and relationship toolkit:

Is this a good time? To ensure you have your partner's undivided attention when you want to discuss an important subject or your partner appears to be pre-occupied, ask: "*Is this a good time?*" This technique is also effective when you make a call and you're unsure if this is an opportune time for the person you called to talk with you. If you ask this simple question prior to beginning your conversation, you respect your partner's time and afford your partner an opportunity to establish a better time to discuss the topic, thereby giving you his/her undivided attention.

That doesn't work for me is a diplomatic way of establishing a different or opposing position that is contrary to what your partner has said or suggested. It also tactfully communicates your opposing point of view without being obnoxious or confrontational.

What I heard you say followed by a restatement or paraphrase, in your own words, of what you heard your partner say. This option provides you the opportunity to seek clarification and to ensure you both have the same understanding. On occasion you may have to re-state, clarify and discuss the topic several times. However, it presents a non-confrontational way of asking for clarification and stating your understanding of what your partner said.

I would like a do over. With these words you're telling your partner that you want an opportunity to re-state, re-phrase, or completely re-do whatever you said or did that didn't come off as you had intended. The operative word here is intended. By requesting a do-over you have an opportunity to start again.

I can really understand why you feel that way and I may not agree with you. Empathy in understanding without agreement is what is implied here. You may understand why your partner has taken a position on a certain issue/matter even though you don't agree with him/her.

You don't say? This old-school response to a statement is what my parents used to express acknowledgement. Back in the day, it was used quite often when my grandparents or mother were engaged as listeners with friends. The phrase, *you don't say,* permitted the listener to remain actively engaged in the conversation without necessarily agreeing or disagreeing with the speaker. The expression was a cleaver form of communication that allowed the listener to remain neutral yet appear as though they were attentive to the speaker and connected to the conversation.

Communications Questions And Answers

Question	Answer
1. Why do couples still have problems **understanding** one another even though they are talking to each other?	Couples often **talk** to one another yet they don't **understand** one another. The primary issue is not about talking; it's about listening. Listening is more than just hearing. Listening is the understanding of the message beyond your partner's words. It's also showing compassion and acknowledging to your partner that *you get it.*
	The remedy is for the receiver to listen wholeheartedly and then provide feedback based on his/her interpretation of what is being said. Ekhart Tolle expresses this best when he says, *"When listening to another person, don't just listen with your mind, listen with your whole body."*
2. What are the *Morse Code of Relationship* Communication Tips?	Representation: Ensure that you accurately present (represent) exactly what you want to convey. Clearly convey your message.
	Timing: Consider not only how but when you deliver the message. If you're addressing a delicate issue, be sensitive to the time and environment.
	Intention: Your intention must be genuine. Alternative motives used to manipulate your partner are inappropriate. Just don't do it.
3. What techniques can I immediately use to alter my mindset and become a better communicator with my partner?	• Transform your mindset and improve your communications with your partner. • Appreciate that your partner does not necessarily feel the same way you do. Your partner is entitled to his/her opinion, just as you are. • Listen. Be respectful. Give mate benefit of doubt. • Be mindful. Don't dwell on the past or the future. • Don't hesitate to sincerely say, *"I'm sorry.. I love you....I forgive you."*

Platinum Sex Rule
Win - Win Sex

Chapter 5: The Platinum Sex Rule
Win-Win Sex

> *Sex is not a mechanical act that fails for lack of technique, and it is not a performance by the male for the audience of the female.*
>
> *It is a continuum of attraction that extends from the simplest conversation and the most innocent touching through the act of coitus.*
>
> Garrison Keillor

Step 5 in *The Couples Cure™ Book, Mastering the Art of Relationships in 7 Easy Steps* lays the foundation to permit you and your partner to enjoy the mutual benefits of intimacy and sex. **The Platinum Sex Rule** is perhaps one of the easiest of the 7 steps to implement and fastest to yield results on your journey to mastering your relationship puzzle. In addition, Step 5 is fun because it involves broaching unchartered territory.

You're more than half way through this book and the process of revitalizing your relationship. Now that you've made adjustments and changes in your mindset and attitude, it is time to continue to put the relationship puzzle together by exploring the unchartered territory of **The Platinum Sex Rule**. It could be just what you and your partner need to rejuvenate the intimacy in your relationship.

"What the heck is The Platinum Sex Rule?" you ask. *"How do I get it? Is it good? Is it legal? Can we discuss The Platinum Sex Rule in mixed company? Is it PG or X rated?"* You may also want to know: *"What needs to be done to ensure my intimate relationship is based on the Platinum Sex Rule?"*

Read on, you'll soon see how one little phrase consisting of six words can transform you and your relationship. In fact, if you and your partner are committed to an unwavering effort, Step 5 can help you transform your life. First, a little history about what I encountered as I prepared to write this chapter on *The Platinum Sex Rule*.

The Road To Platinum Sex

I'd be remiss if I did not address the topic of sex and sensuality in this book. I am always astounded at the number of self-help books written about relationships and the number of authors who fail to include sex and sensuality when they make recommendations about relationships.

In addition to authors' reluctance to address the topic of sex and sensuality, I also found that same reluctance with the majority of people I talked with. Nearly 500 people openly shared their opinions and experiences about healthy, fulfilling relationships. Yet they remained tight-lipped on the topic of sex and sensuality.

What I found most fascinating is that men and women hesitate to bring up the topic of sex. All other relationship themes were candidly discussed, but not sex, nor sensuality. Often, I'd ask, *"Does sex play a part in a healthy, fulfilling relationship? Does the quality, frequency, engagement and type of sex enter the equation when calculating happy partnerships?"*

In 98% of my discussions with men, women, young, old, married, never married, divorced, straight, LGBTQ, and different religious and ethnic backgrounds, I found people were reluctant to discuss sex. The topic of sex appeared to be akin to discussing the plague or some other terrible and taboo disease that should not be talked about. I did not understand why. As a matter of fact, I had to literally pull the subject out in some instances. As time went on, I conscientiously made a decision to not bring the subject into the conversation just to see what would happen. The resulting fact was this: If I didn't bring it up, only 2% of those people with whom I had conversations ever broached the subject.

The conclusion is that most people just don't talk about sex. It stands to reason why there are a high number of sexless partnerships, marriages and sexually dysfunctional relationships. It's one thing if a partnership is sexless by choice, design or physical limitations. It's a completely different situation if one of the partners no longer wants to engage in sex.

So I ask you: "If you were one of the almost 500 people who shared your opinion with me about relationships and what constitutes healthy, fulfilling relationships, would you initiate the topic of sex? Or would you wait until I asked the question?" If your answer was No and you would not initiate the topic, ask yourself this question: "Why wouldn't I casually talk about sex? Why is sex and sensuality, even in a safe wholesome environment, such a forbidden subject?"

Well, a blatant omission of the topic of sex simply isn't going to happen in this book. Not on my watch! I know the gravity this topic carries in almost all relationships, regardless of whether the sex is considered good, bad or non-existent. Sex and sensuality are especially critical when talking about how to remedy the issues couples and partners face in the effort to find a solution to their relationship puzzle.

Platinum Sex Rule: The Origin

Step 5 in mastering the art of relationships is understanding, sharing and maintaining the benefits of *The Platinum Sex Rule* and *The Win-Win Sex Formula* for relationships.

What exactly is *The Platinum Sex Rule* and what is platinum sex?

First, recognize the significance and qualities of platinum. In the world of chemistry, platinum is a precious metal. It is a highly valued commodity. When compared to gold, platinum is more dense, stronger and therefore more expensive than gold in volume.

In contemporary terms, platinum is used to denote an esteemed status or achievement. In the record industry, a platinum record is more prestigious than a gold record. In the credit card industry, the platinum credit card is the top notch, highest level credit card — indicative of the ultimate status symbol for living the good life.

As I distilled data gathered from conversations about committed relationships, one concept came to mind. The vocabulary choices included words like prized, rare and extraordinary to describe the ultimate in sex, the requirements for sensuality and intimacy. Equally important was that both partners were willing participants and were in agreement as to the expectations and the outcome(s). In my mind and without oversimplification, those terms, concepts, and explanations channeled the best, the highest rated, the ultimate attainment in sex, sensuality and intimacy. Thus, the coining of the phrase: **The Platinum Sex Rule**.

To ensure the same understanding in the context of *The Couples Cure™ Book, Mastering the Art of Relationships in 7 Easy Steps*, I've included several clarifying definitions and explanations.

Sex, Sensuality & Intimacy Defined

Sex. Most dictionaries don't address the subject of the physical act of sex. There are extended explanations about the classifications of the male and female genders under the definition of sex. However the physical act itself is limited to the terms of: sexual intercourse, the activity of having sex, or sexual activity, specifically intercourse.

It appears that there really ought to be more expanded definitions as it relates to sexual activities. If the major dictionaries in the world can't define and explain something so significant to relationships, it's no wonder that partners and couples have difficulty discussing the subject.

Sensual/Sensuality. Webster defines sensual as: *relating to or consisting in the gratification of the senses or the indulgence of appetite.* Another web definition addresses sensual as *relating to, devoted to, or producing physical or sexual pleasure.*

Intimacy. Intimacy is defined by Webster as *pertaining to or indicative of one's deepest nature; close associations, contact, or familiarity; warm friendship; informal warmth or privacy..* Dictionary.com says, *close, familiar, and loving physical relationship with another person or group.*

The Platinum Sex Rule Guidelines

As *The Couples Cure™ Lady* and life coach, my task is to provide you and your partner with tools and wisdom to help you navigate Step 5, **The Platinum Sex Rule**. The following pages contain guidelines to assist you and your partner in a committed partnership to open the dialogue about your sensuality, intimacy and sex within your relationship.

To facilitate the process I have developed two Platinum Sex Rule worksheets. Worksheet 1 - *The Partner's Agreement* provides a number of statements to which you and your partner will both want to agree to follow in this exercise. Worksheet 2 - *Platinum Sex Rule Discussion* will help you describe and then share your thoughts about your sexual relationship with your partner. (For your convenience, The Platinum Sex Rule worksheets in a PDF format are also available at TheCouplesCureBook.com.)

Worksheet 1 – The Partner's Agreement

It is imperative that both you and your partner read and agree to the statements in *The Partner's Agreement*. First, I suggest that each partner carefully read and consider whether they concur with each statement in the agreement. If there are statements on which you and your partner cannot agree, please be sure to discuss these with each other before proceeding to Worksheet 2. If necessary, you may rewrite the agreement statements to best suit your relationship or unique situation. Without such an agreement, implementation of Worksheet 2 - *Platinum Sex Rule Discussion* may be unsuccessful.

Worksheet 1: The Partner's Agreement

> *Instructions: Each partner should carefully read, consider and agree to the following statements. If there are statements on which you and your partner cannot agree, it is important that you discuss these with each other before proceeding to Worksheet 2; and, if necessary, you may rewrite the agreement statements to best suit your relationship.*

_____ I am committed to do the work required to enhance my relationship with my partner.

_____ My expectations are adjusted to facilitate achieving both my and my partner's desired, positive outcome.

_____ I seek first to understand my partner; then I seek to be understood by my partner.

_____ I am careful not to criticize my partner's responses or sexual prowess (or lack thereof).

_____ I am an active listener. I am a willing receiver and recipient in this conversation.

_____ I initiate the conversation with my partner.

_____ I understand that in committed relationships, sex manifests itself in any number of ways.

_____ I embrace the Garrison Keillor theory that sex has multiple stages and phases: *"Sex is a continuum of attraction that extends from the simplest conversation and the most innocent touching through the act of coitus."*

_____ I actively listen to my partner's responses to the questions in Worksheet 2 - *Platinum Sex Rule Discussion*.

Worksheet 2: Platinum Sex Rule Discussion

Worksheet 2 – *Platinum Sex Rule Discussion* provides a systematic, focused and organized plan to constructively discuss the individual circumstances regarding your personal sexual relationship with your partner.

First, I suggest that you and your partner independently complete Worksheet 2 - *Platinum Sex Rule Discussion*. In completing this worksheet, answer as truthfully, directly, and specifically as possible. Once both you and your partner have answered these questions independently, set aside a time and place to begin to share your answers -- a time when there will be no interruptions or distractions and a place where you feel safe and secure.

In completing this worksheet, be sure to take as much time as needed to cover all of the topics. Remember: This worksheet does NOT have to be completed in a single session; in fact, in most instances, you may find it helpful to break up the discussions to address one or two topics at a time.

At first you and your partner may have difficulty sharing your responses. This is to be expected, so don't despair. You'll find this discussion easier and easier over time.

Remember: Every couple is different.
Every couple has unique requirements.
Every couple needs to determine what level of sex,
sensuality, and intimacy they desire and
what works for them and their relationship.

So, relax and enjoy this exciting exploration and experimentation! Be as creative as you wish, trying to "think out of the box" as you evolve and experiment with different approaches to achieving your own unique "Win-Win" sexual relationship.

Worksheet 2: Platinum Sex Rule Discussion

Instructions: Each partner should independently complete the discussion topics listed below. Be as truthful, direct, and specific as possible. Once you and your partner have completed your responses, set aside a time and place to begin to share your answers. Take as much time as needed. This worksheet does not have to be completed in a single session; in most instances, it may be helpful to break up the sessions by addressing one or two topics at a time. Remember, every couple is different, has unique needs, and will evolve a unique way of creating intimacy.

Teach Your Partner How to Pleasure You

What are the three most pleasurable experiences you have had with your partner in the last year, whether or not these experiences are directly related to sex? What are the three most enjoyable ways that you like to provide pleasure to your partner?

_____

_____

_____

_____

_____

_____

Intimacy

Pertaining to or indicative of one's deepest nature. Close association, contact, or familiarity -- warm friendship. Usually affectionate or loving personal relationship with another person. Not necessarily linked to intercourse or coitus.

What Works? What Doesn't Work?

_____

_____

_____

_____

_____

_____

Foreplay

Erotic stimulation preceding sexual intercourse; physical, sexual actions (such as kissing and touching) that couples do with each other before they have sexual intercourse.

What's Pleasurable? What's Not So Pleasurable?

_____

_____

_____

_____

_____

_____

Kissing

What's Pleasurable? What's Not So Pleasurable?

_____

_____

_____

_____

_____

_____

Hygiene
Conditions or practices conducive to good health. Cleanliness.

What's Pleasurable? What's Not So Pleasurable?

_____

_____

_____

_____

_____

_____

Sexual Intercourse

What's Pleasurable? What's Not So Pleasurable?

_____

_____

_____

_____

_____

_____

_____

Tantric Sex
A spiritual and prolonged sexual process of cultivating
a more fulfilling, loving relationship with or without intercourse.

What Works? What Doesn't Work?

_____

_____

_____

_____

_____

_____

Consensual, No-Sex Relationship
Mutual agreement between partners not to have sexual intercourse, sometimes due to health or other issues/concerns.

What Works? What Doesn't Work?

_____

_____

_____

_____

_____

_____

Other Related Topics
Other related topics that you'd like to discuss with your partner, whether or not these relate to sexual pleasure.

What's Pleasurable? What's Not So Pleasurable?
What Works? What Doesn't Work?

_____

_____

_____

_____

_____

_____

Resolving Challenges and Issues

As you undertake this exploration of your sexual and intimate relationship with your partner, you may encounter a number of challenges or issues. It may be uncomfortable at first to having a compassionate, frank, and open discussion leading to a more pleasurable and meaningful sexual life. Below, we discuss some of the most common challenges encountered by couples on this journey. These challenges, issues, and the recommendations may help you achieve Win-Win Sex using *The Platinum Sex Rule, The Win-Win Formula.*

Your Partner Doesn't Want To Discuss Your Challenges. If and when you partner doesn't want to talk about the challenges that you experience in your sexual encounters and intimacy, you've got problems. Lack of desire to discuss intimacy issues is not an impossible situation; however, it will take effort. Those problems are greater than can be handled by *The Couples Cure™ Book, The Couples Cure Lady,* or *The Couple's Cure™ System.* When the status of your sex and intimacy reaches the state where there is no communication, you need to seek counsel from a licensed and trained professional.

Gabriela and I met at a workshop in Santa Clara. We soon began talking and exchanged the traditional niceties about our professions and where we are from. It turns out that Gabriela was from Brazil. She was quite open about the topic of her sex life with her husband, Rolando. He was a small business owner; she was a stay-at-home mom. The reason she was so able to freely discuss the true nature of their intimacy and lack thereof is because they had divorced. Even though they were married some 16 years and had three children, the main issue was that there was no communication in their relationship. By Gabriela's account, *"It doesn't matter what the subject is. We simply do not communicate when there are issues in our relationship. The issue is that Rolando simply does not want to discuss anything that he thinks is unpleasant. So we have gone on for years without communicating.*"

There were numerous opportunities for open dialogue. However, they did not communicate about Rolando's extramarital affair. They did not communicate when Gabriela lost their baby as a result of a miscarriage. And they did not communicate in an attempt to resolve any of their intimacy problems. Gabriela had just shut down. Yet Rolando wanted to continue to have sexual relations with her, not understanding why she wasn't willing to take a more active part in their intimacy. There was so little communication that they got to a point where there was no sex, no intimacy at all, and the union ultimately ended in divorce.

Keep in mind that this is a simplified explanation of a more complex situation by one of the partners. However, know that the facts are real. In order to have and maintain a lasting relationship there must be communication. In my conversations with both men and women about failure to communicate regarding intimacy and sexual dissatisfaction, the number one reason for straying outside the partnership is that one partner or the other felt a major void in the need to communicate. Both men and women said they needed validation. The other person made them feel special, wanted and desired and, in some cases, loved.

Quite the contrary is illustrated in the movie, *Under the Tuscan Sun.* Diane Lane stars in this film, set in the Tuscan Valley, Italy. One of the subplots of the movie is about a young couple, Pawel, a young Polish worker and his Italian girlfriend. Pawel could not speak any Italian and his girlfriend could not speak Polish. Yet they were able to communicate through the universal aphrodisiac -- communications -- using their eyes, arm gestures and body language. This young couple was unable to initially converse with one another using their birth languages; yet they were able to communicate adequately enough to fall in love and ultimately convince their parents — albeit both were just teenagers -- to stand by them and support their marriage.

It's Too Frustrating. You've tried some form of the process before and you know it doesn't work. You feel it's frustrating and not worth the energy. You also think it's tiring. It's too much work. It's too much effort. Once again, you're making excuses. You can either put forth the effort, or not. No more reasons. Your reasons are simply excuses. So the bottom line is this: If you truly want to make your relationship work, it'll take effort on your part. Be the change you want to see.

It Makes Me Vulnerable. The process of admitting you have an issue and that you don't currently enjoy the benefits of platinum sex makes you vulnerable. I get it. However, know that the first step to correcting any situation begins with vulnerability and admitting you have an issue. Similar to addressing any other challenge in life, i.e., alcoholism, drug addiction, eating disorders and the like, the chief motivator in the process is to first admit you've got a challenge. In admitting you have a problem, you make yourself vulnerable. Even more beneficial is to open yourself to beginning the process of repairing, healing, and changing the behavior which will also change your life.

My Partner Is Not Willing or Has Turned Off To Sex. Another challenge is how to start the healing process to get your relationship back on track. Even though you're apprehensive that your partner may not be willing or has no inclination to improve the sexual and intimacy aspects of your relationship, ask your partner: Do you want to make the sexual and intimacy aspects of our relationship work? The real answer should be a resounding *Yes*. If the response is anything other than *Yes*, then the issue may not necessarily be sex at all. However, the net result plays out in disrupting your intimacy and sexual activities. The lack of desire or unwillingness to engage with your partner needs to be resolved before you can move forward.

Let me take a moment to clarify a couple of things relative to sex. I've often heard men say that their partners are no longer interested in sex. That may or may not be true. Many women suffer from physical injury, impairment or physiological changes driven by a reduction in hormonal levels which directly relate to the desire for sex. Similarly, men may avoid sexual intercourse because they fear that they cannot perform up to standard, whether or not that standard is realistic. Many men, especially as they age, are affected by erectile dysfunction, sometimes due to lower testosterone levels, prostate cancer, or emotional issues. For both men and women, these conditions may require medical or psychological intervention. Once the physiological and physical impairment has been resolved, resumption of healthy intimacy and sex can become quite normal.

In addition, I've discovered that women and men sometimes lose their desire for sex with their current partner. This is not an indication that your partner is not interested in sex at all. Given the opportunity to engage in sex with another partner, the woman or man may present a completely different picture. Why is that? The primary reason is that sex may have become a routine, uninteresting, matter-of-fact obligatory behavior – *"Because I'm supposed to."*

For women, so much of the emotional connectivity associated with sex is generated by activities and influences that have absolutely nothing to do with sex. Some women tend to be more emotional than men. In the majority of cases, a woman's sexual arousal and interest in levels of intimacy are based on her emotional connections with and to her partner. For many men, their sexual arousal and interest is often triggered by more visual and tactile cues.

Partners Differ In The Timing of Sex After Arguments

Sometimes partners have differences concerning how quickly to engage in sex after a heated argument. The myth is that to engage in sex soon after an argument will make things OK. The truth is that women tend to need more time than men to recover from an argument before having sex. They need time to refocus and redirect their emotions before they are ready to reengage. Men, on the other hand, sometimes simply need to be able to say, *"OK. I get it, I'm sorry. I heard what you said."* For them, the argument or disagreement is then over and they may say, *"Let's move on."* which means, *"Let's have sex."* This is not an indictment of either women nor men; rather, it highlights the need for both partners to be sensitive to the timing of sexual interactions. When couples take their partner's personality and needs into account, they have an opportunity to respond more appropriately. This allows for them to enjoy increased intimacy, including Platinum Sex.

A Win-Win Formula for Dedicated Couples

The *Win-Win Formula* allows both partners in a dedicated relationship to enjoy mutually-gratifying sensuality and sexual experiences. Any issue can be worked through if you and your partner are willing to address them.

Remember:
You get out of your sex life what you put into it. If your relationship is worth keeping, then do what needs to be done to enhance your sex life. It's well worth the effort.

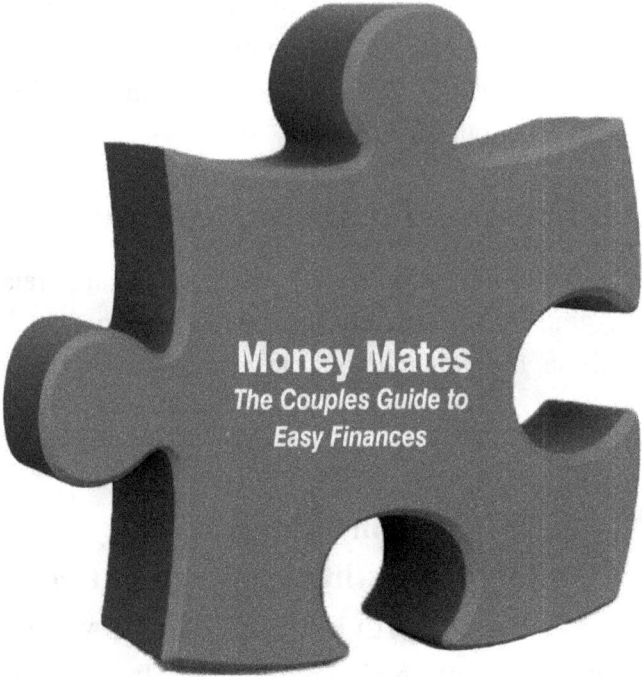

Money Mates
The Couples Guide to
Easy Finances

Chapter 6: Money Mates

The Couples Guide To Easy Finances

> *Life is not all about money. It's more about relationships.*
>
> Michael Patrick

Step 6 in *The Couples Cure™ Book, Mastering the Art of Relationships in 7 Easy Steps* is **Money Mates**. This chapter on **Money Mates** emphasizes the essential necessity for intimate, long-term partners to have similar beliefs and a common philosophical approach to the management of their money and assets.

The purpose of **Money Mates** is to provide thought-provoking fiscal relationship tools. In the event you and your partner have a desire to move toward more fiscal compatibility, **Money Mates** provides the ideal support for your financial transition. These fiscal tools can offer you and your partner practical options to enhance your financial relationship. Your partnership can be enriched as you both continue to develop and cultivate your relationship as solid financial companions and **Money Mates.**

This Chapter on **Money Mates** includes several scenarios about couples, their assets and financial issues. These scenarios discuss the methodology partners use to manage financial resources. They each conclude with thought provoking questions for you and your partner to reflect upon and discuss how each of you would react under similar circumstances.

Money Mates also offers you and your mate the opportunity to explore the importance of each partners' values and the compatibility of your financial blueprints.

In addition, **Money Mates** will share the details of a successful "financial breakup" of a loving couple. This couple struggled for sometime and came close to dissolving their relationship. The culprit of the near dissolution was the vast difference in their financial blueprint, values, spending behavior and money management styles. Read on to discover what one couple did to salvage and enhance their partnership.

Management of partner's resources is unique to every couple. Therefore, this Chapter does not direct you and your partner toward any financial practice. It does not attempt to persuade you or your mate how to best manage your finances or who should be responsible for household resources. Also know that this chapter does not address investment tactics, accounting principles, how to generate income or banking procedures.

Money Mates will nonetheless continue to share the wisdom from hundreds of healthy happy couples who have confirmed the best financial relationships features.

Culprits That Cause Financial Woes

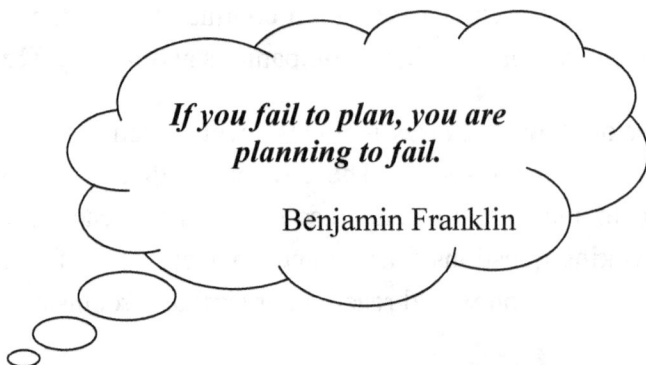

If you fail to plan, you are planning to fail.

Benjamin Franklin

Some couples have financial difficulty because they don't share the same financial philosophy. Other partnerships encounter monetary challenges

98

caused by a simple failure to discuss and establish a solid financial management plan. Benjamin Franklin's quote about the lack of planning is attributable to major issues in intimate relationships. Couples' financial woes are in the top three categories and reasons for separation and divorce. Money issues are third only to communications (irreconcilable differences) and sex.

There are times when your partnership's financial challenges have nothing to do with the amount of money made and brought into the household. Rather, the offenders or financial issues often stem from a lack of discussions and planning about how to handle whatever the shared income and circumstances happen to be.

Partnership financial difficulties occur when couples:

- May not have the same monetary values or financial blueprint.

- Don't know how to manage their money spending and savings.

- Fail to establish priorities of needs vs. wants.

- Are unable or unwilling to stick with their budget (provided there is a budget).

- Suffer a significant change in income, i.e., layoff or unemployment of one of the partners.

- Have unexpected medical bills.

- Experience an unexpected death or illness in the family.

- Make bad investments.

When To Make Financial Adjustments

When is the best time to make financial adjustments? Perhaps the story below will shed some light on the answer.

Lucy and Robert were both 40-something when they married. Lucy had one prior marriage and one child from that union; her son lived with her former husband. This was Robert's first marriage. They both worked in the entertainment industry. Each had been with their respective company for more than 20 years. They also had similar incomes. Each had a 401 savings and investment accounts. Money did not appear to be an issue.

When they married, Lucy and Robert agreed to a 50-50 split of their outstanding monthly obligations. The net result was a fairly even distribution of financial responsibilities for both Lucy and Robert. Early in their marriage, payments were regularly made on their mortgages, the cars, the boat, utilities, etc. Life was good. Their savings flourished. Their credit scores were near 800. They lived quite the lifestyle as a young, affluent fun-loving couple.

Life happens. Things change. Robert and Lucy were impacted by the financial downturn in 2008. Lucy was laid off after 20 years. She was able to draw unemployment/lay off checks for a period of time. Lucy went through most of her savings during the next five years attempting to hold up her end of their 50-50 split of monthly obligations. After all, they made an agreement at the time they were married. Eventually she ran out of money. She was unable to continue to pay her half of the monthly obligations.

Lucy and Robert didn't talk about the change in Lucy's income after the layoff. Lucy did not bring the subject up. Apparently Robert was unwilling to discuss the matter.

Lucy's investment account had been pilfered due to her frequent withdrawals. In addition, she was heavily taxed on the early withdrawals. Robert and Lucy suffered a significant drop in their FICO credit scores. Several years later Robert and Lucy divorced. They split their remaining assets.

Early in their marriage, Robert and Lucy had a financial plan. Initially, they were financially compatible and had a workable agreement. They failed to prepare for an alternative or back-up plan.

Discuss this scenario with your partner. Would you have approached their financial situation differently if you were Lucy? What would you have done differently if you were Robert if anything? What would you and your partner do to preserve the relationship?

Perhaps this is a good time to look at your own financial situation. Does your plan need to be tweaked or adjusted? Do you have an alternative plan in the event of a major financial shift in your income level?

Fiscal Values & Communications

Your values play an enormous role in determining who you are, what you believe, and how you behave. Your values also affect your financial blueprint and behavior. Your values are another name for your deep core principles and innermost feelings. Your values are the nucleus of who you are. They are principles that you hold to be of worth in your life. People often confuse values with morals. Values are not chosen. They are intrinsic to who you are (as discussed on the chapter on Mindset). The closer you and your partner are when you share the same values, maintain similar belief systems, and lifestyle principles, the more likely you are to have open, candid discussions and to have a long-lasting and happy relationship. That was not the case with Miguel and Maria.

Miguel and Maria, a married couple I've known for years, have very different values. Miguel is a sculptor; his wife, Maria, works for an insurance agency. They now live in different homes, in different states. I shudder to even call them a couple. They are so different. Miguel's values, goals and personal motivation are all driven by his need to create beautiful sculpted pieces and express his artistic talents through his work. Miguel has never appeared to be concerned about a secure future for his family. He doesn't appear to be a good manager of money either. Quite frankly, I suspect that neither financial freedom nor financial independence has ever entered his mind. Miguel asked me, during one of my impromptu interviews about relationships, *"Why can't Maria understand my need to be creative? Why doesn't she get the fact that my purpose on earth is to be a sculptor...?"* After more than fifteen minutes of complaining about Maria, he went on to say, *"Maria just doesn't get it. She just doesn't understand what I'm all about."*

Maria on the other hand comes from a conservative background. She's the consummate saver and wants to stay on top of and control their discretionary funds. Maria wants to ensure they have a comfortable retirement and relatively uncomplicated life during their golden years. On the contrary, Miguel is a true artiste! He has a heart of gold. He buys clothes and owns all the latest electronic toys. Meanwhile Miguel drives his wife nuts with his carefree spending habits. According to Maria, *"He has little regard for the future."* They're both in their fifties, and they've never owned a home. For the past twenty-five years, they've been apartment dwellers. Miguel has had a variety of jobs with different companies—mostly part time so that he can devote time to his work as sculptor in the evening and on weekends.

It became clear to me that Miguel and Maria never openly discussed their long-term expectations prior to marriage. And now, they are light years apart in their values, beliefs, physical locations as well as spiritual connections as a married couple. Both Maria and Miguel are at the stage in life when they are considering what to do as they approach retirement. Maria is beginning to think about making the transition from being full time employed to retiring. She confided in me that she thought her knight in shining armor would take care of her so she could retire early. To the contrary, her knight in shining armor thinks that they are partners and should both continue to work—especially since there are no savings, no retirement, and no visible means to change their current financial condition. Their values, goals, and long-term aspirations have never been on the same page, let alone being similar or even consistent; yet, Maria and Miguel never sat down to discuss what they wanted in the later years in life. No doubt, when they first fell in love and decided to get married, there was little thought given to the significance of values or dreams for the future. Miguel and Maria probably didn't talk about nor ask about each other's values. I wonder if they will ever get back together.

Unfortunately many people are not willing to do what is required to preserve their relationship. These couples refuse to put forth the effort to rejuvenate their relationship and learn or use the skills necessary to keep their partnership.

Men and women spend hundreds of thousands of dollars on their cars—the wheel rims, new and slick paint jobs, complete renovation of the interior—substituting leather for the old knock-off leather looking vinyl. Yet, they're not willing to invest the same anount of time or energy in their relationships as they do with some of their material possessions.

Your Financial Blueprint

Everyone has a financial personality. What's yours? Before answering, consider how would you respond to the following money management questions:

- How do you feel about amassing a large sum of money?

- What are your values and beliefs about money?

- How to you feel about securing your future?

- What happens if/when money becomes scarce in your household?

- Are you a spender or a saver? Is your partner a saver or spender or somewhere in between?

Also, consider the positive and negative interactions that shaped your thoughts and relationships with money as you were growing up? Did you come from a family with ample money that splurged now and again to allow you to enjoy those special occasions without guilt? Or, did you or your partner grow up in a household where money was tight?

How compatible is your and your partner's financial relationship? Do you perceive money as the ultimate negotiating tool? Do you use money in your intimate relationship as a power tool to negotiate what you want? Are you completely honest about money in your current relationship?

After answering these questions, identify the top three to five money management subjects you would like to discuss with your partner to enhance your Money Mates compatibility. Engage your partner to identify their top three to five money management subjects as well. Preface your discussion with a compassionate request and the intention to increase your success levels for a continued healthy and long-term relationship. Some areas that may be particularly relevant to your and your partner's financial relationship may include:

- Savings & Investments

- Annual Income

- Ensuring a Secure Future

- Credit Worthiness and Your FICO Scores

- Who Controls the Checkbook

- Joint Account vs. Separate Accounts

- Significant Debts

- Bill Paying, Records Organization and Attention to Details

Below are three stories illustrating ways in which some couples handled their financial relationships. Two of these stories describe how couples failed to successfully handle their financial relationship; the third illustrates how a committed couple managed to successfully renegotiate a failing financial relationship.

Story #1. The Ego Buster

Jonathan married Alexis who was 10 years his junior. Jonathan was in the retail industry. As a young, bright and capable young man, he was promoted quickly up the corporate ladder. Jonathan's income was more than adequate to support himself and his new bride who was in college and wanted to pursue a career in law. Early in their marriage they made a joint decision that Alexis would continue college to get her bachelor's degree and then a law school degree.

At that time, Jonathan's salary was the primary source of income. He controlled the money and assets. Most of the time during their early marriage, Alexis was in school. Occasionally, she took part-time jobs to help pay off some of her law school expenses. Jonathan and Alexis were content with their financial arrangement while she was a student.

After law school, passing the bar and her internship, Alexis became a criminal defense attorney. Alexis was a good criminal defense attorney and, after a number of years, her income surpassed Jonathan's.

Jonathan had a problem. His ego was the issue. He knew it and he recognized his shortcomings. Jonathan assumed his wife would pursue a career in corporate law. He also reluctantly acknowledged his wife's love of criminal law, the excitement of live representation in criminal defense cases and the substantial income of attorneys in that discipline.

What he didn't anticipate was that he would be unable to manage his feelings. Jonathan claimed to be old school. He had difficulty with a reversal of income roles. In his mind, the man was always supposed to be the partner who made the most money. He simply didn't and couldn't accept that his young wife made more money.

Money was never an issue for Alexis. It mattered not who brought in what amount into the household. Family money was combined income in Alexis' mind. Unfortunately, they quarreled constantly. Jonathan admitted that most of the time he would pick fights with Alexis about frivolous issues. The fights would allow him to feel as though he had some control. Jonathan did not want to seek counseling. Men, according to Jonathan, don't go to therapists; they resolve their own problems. Jonathan filed for divorce citing irreconcilable differences. Alexis didn't refute the divorce. She was exhausted and tired of quarreling. They still remain friends.

Based on this story, there are several issues for you and your partner to think about and discuss: How would you handle the situation differently? What would you have done if the roles were reversed and Alexis worked while Jonathan went to school? What if this situation occurred with a same sex couple? Would you and your partner consider seeing a therapist or seeking guidance from a relationship coach?

Story #2. The Illusive FICO & Inadvertent Oversights

Sven and Helga were in their mid 50s and had similar Nordic backgrounds. Sven was a pharmaceutical salesman, Helga was a fitness and yoga trainer. Both appeared to be financially stable.

Sven lived in an apartment, with no maintenance; and was constantly on the road. He was a great salesman and made lots of money. He was the perfect gentleman and swept Helga off her feet.

Helga was conservative regarding money management and had stellar credit. She owned and was proud of her small home. Her income as a fitness manager had to be conserved. In spite of her smaller income, she was adamant about saving.

Sven and Helga met in November, had a whirlwind romance and were married in December. The happy couple moved into Helga's home and began their new life together. She immediately added his name to the deed of trust for her home.

In January they filed their Federal Tax Forms as a married couple. In February Helga's car broke down. They decided to buy a new car. The auto dealership required a standard credit check for new vehicles.

Helga had stellar credit. Sven's credit scores ranged between 450 and 500 depending on the credit bureau. Sven and Helga were dumbfounded; they had no idea his credit score was so low. He travelled a lot, hardly having time to read the mail, let alone pay bills. Yes, he had been late with monthly payments on several credit cards. Five years ago, he had his car repossessed. He may have been in default status on one of his prior loans. but had no idea his credit was bad.

Helga was livid with the credit situation. When she started to investigate Sven's background, she was in shock. She found that Sven had been married and never divorced. He had an adult child that he saw occasionally. Sven failed to mention these facts, along with his low credit score to Helga.

Although Helga dearly loved Sven, she felt she couldn't trust him. She wasn't sure what else he might have inadvertently neglected to disclose. Helga divorced Sven and spent the next seven years trying to straighten out her financial records.

What lessons did you learn from this couple's financial woes? How would you and your partner have done things differently? Was there something that could have been done to save the marriage? Was it worth saving?

Story #3. The Successful Financial Breakup

Sasha and Portia had a good, healthy relationship that had taken a turn. The challenge was Portia's relationship with money and her spending habits.

Sasha and Portia had been together for 12 years. Sasha was beginning to experience growing frustration in the relationship. She immediately knew that it was because of their financial issues.

Sasha was a chief financial officer at a manufacturing company. Because of her education, experience and background, most of her life was spent dealing in the financial arena. Sasha was not label conscious nor did she care about the latest fashions or hot clothing trends. Sasha by her own description was a practical individual. She took pride in the fact that she was rather conservative and very good with financial figures.

Portia, on the other hand, had a very different background; Portia's life revolved around interior design. Her style and color coordination, her selection of fabrics--everything about her emanated high style and design.

Sasha and Portia had a joint checking account. Portia constantly updated her wardrobe. Portia often attempted to explain the difference between Prada and Coach to her partner. Portia went so far as to max out the American Express cards and was busted. Sasha was furious with Portia.

All other aspects of their relationship seemed to be going well. Unfortunately their financial situation left them stressed out or angry with the other for long periods of time.

Sasha took the lead. She used a spreadsheet so the gravity of their financial situation and their debt was perfectly clear. She then drafted a financial plan – it was called "The Financial Breakup." The bottom line of the financial breakup plan was to renegotiate, divide their expenses and completely revamp the financial structure of their relationship.

The following are the terms of their Plan:

The Financial Breakup

The Goal:

The goal is to take individual responsibility for debt and spending to increase awareness and decrease stress.

The Bottom Line:

Total Revolving Installment Debt Owed – $103,186

Total Monthly Revolving Installment Debt – $2,798

The History:

In July and August 2007, Sasha contributed $14,588 toward debt reduction. Portia will contribute $14,588 toward debt reduction from Macy's IRA. The debt to be reduced will be jointly allocated revolving debt to include Sears, Fidelity, Target and Shell.

*　*　*

The Plan:

From this day forward, Sasha and Portia will be solely responsible for the debts assigned.

They will be jointly (50%) responsible for future household and miscellaneous expenses.

Sasha will invoice Portia twice monthly for her expenses and assume responsibility for the payment.

Portia will assume ownership of the existing checking and savings accounts (formally removing Sasha).

Sasha will open a new individual checking account.

Portia will be removed as an authorized user on the following accounts: Neiman Marcus and Shell.

Sasha will be removed as an authorized user from Portia's American Express and Nordstrom.

Dated: _____

Signatures _____ & _____

*　*　*

The Financial Breakup process took about three weeks. It was indeed a financial breakup. Sasha went to the bank that day and immediately started their plan for debt reduction. Their relationship improved significantly.

When I asked about the process and whether or not she thought it was good, Sasha said that initially they were both very upset. When I asked what she would do differently, she said, "It was actually okay and, considering all circumstances, it went well and we accomplished our goal."

Sasha also said, "If we had not taken the initiative, we would have been involved with a bankruptcy for our primary home." She also said "I would have insisted that Portia assume some of the financial responsibility. In retrospect, the easiest way to deal with a renegotiation process is to find out what 'the thing is' that is causing the pain."

Six years later she says they both see light at the end of the tunnel.

Pros of a Financial Breakup and Renegotiation
- *Put the plan in writing*
- *Writing provides clarity*
- *It's a constant reminder of what the agreement was*

Cons of a Financial Breakup and Renegotiation
- *It appears to be sterile*
- *It sounds like a formal process*

I'm pleased to report that Sasha and Portia are doing just fine. They're grateful for having a relationship that still works. In this instance, it was an excellent opportunity to renegotiate the terms and budgetary aspects of their financial relationship.

What are your thoughts about the Financial Breakup?

This partnership renegotiation process can be used and applied to any area where a couple experiences difficulties in their relationship.

Sound Financial Management Philosophy

Good financial management is not difficult. Consistent with all prior Chapters in *The Couples Cure™ Book, Mastering the Art of Relationships in 7 Easy Steps*, the first phase to becoming compatible Money Mates is financial clarity. Clarity of your partnership's combined assets can be a significant boost to the transition of your financial relationship. Clarity and a financial plan usually results in more harmony in your relationship.

The second phase is an agreed-upon financial plan that allows you, as a couple, to deal with your current resources, obligations and unexpected circumstances that impact your financial situation.

The amount of money you earn is not necessarily indicative of good financial management. Nor is a small dollar amount in you bank account balance an indication of poor financial management. Maintaining a philosophy of solid financial management involves several basic principles. Fiscally compatible Money Mates ensures that your partnership includes concrete financial management principles: loving communication, consistency, accountability, transparency, values, freedom, and openness:

- Communication: Loving communications are essential to healthy discussions about you and your partner's financial status.

- Consistency: Whatever method you use to ensure you and your partner understand and maintain the same processes and systems

- Accountability: Be responsible for your savings and spending.

- Transparency: Are you both transparent about your spending? Do your spending habits stand the test of scrutiny?

- Values: Strive to reach similar values for a more compatible financial blueprint (even if you have considerable differences).

- Freedom: Power free financial partnerships (void of using money or lack of money to manipulate or control your partner).

- Openness: Willingness to renegotiate the terms of your financial partnership to ensure balance and equitability.

Money Mates, The Couples Guide to Easy Finances, has offered you and your partner the opportunity to explore the importance of your values and the compatibility of your financial blueprint. Your thoughts and behavior (financial or otherwise) are all based on your values. Likewise, the more compatible you and your partner's financial values are, the more likely you'll enjoy a healthy, happy relationship.

Remember:

Management of financial and other resources are unique to every couple. The responsibility always rests with you and your partner to decide what is best for your circumstances and your individual relationship.

Renegotiate
Time for a Re-Do

Chapter 7: Renegotiate
Time For A Re-Do

> *For me, relationship is very important.*
> *I can lose money, but I cannot lose a relationship.*
> *The test is, at the end of a conversation*
> *or a negotiation, both must smile.*
>
> Sunil Mittal

Step 7 is to **Renegotiate** in *The Couples Cure™ Book, Mastering the Art of Relationships in 7 Easy Steps*. Renegotiate is an action verb. It means to negotiate (something) again to change the terms of the first agreement. An alternate definition for renegotiate is to try to reach an agreement or compromise by discussion with others; or find a way over or through (an obstacle or difficult path) when something has been modified.

This chapter should be used to initiate an honest and healthy discussion about the changes in your relationship, and ideally come to a win-win agreement and understanding as you move forward as a couple.

The Foundation To Renegotiate

The purpose of Step 7 is to lay the foundation for you and your partner to renegotiate or re-do the terms of some aspect of your relationship, if necessary. On occasion, you and your partner may have a desire or need to compromise or reach an agreement on some particular facet of your relationship that has changed or is in the process of changing.

This re-do is not designed for the day-to-day challenges and changes you experience. Rather, this chapter serves as a couple's reference tool and provides an opportunity for you to open the channels of communication with your partner when something has changed significantly, and you or your partner feel it's time to discuss or renegotiate.

Life Happens, Things Change

Couples can go years without the need to re-do or renegotiate anything in their relationship. You and your partner may have that kind of partnership. You could be in a relationship or marriage where you rarely have a disagreement. You and your partner may have a life style where only minor shifts have transpired in your partnership during the time you've been together. In addition, there are those congruent relationships where your partner activities or life styles change effortlessly and discussions about the changing nuances are rare. In these unions there may be little need to renegotiate, if at all. That's fine.

Times change, people change,
situations change, relationships change.
The only thing constant is change.
Source Unknown

On the other hand and more typically, life happens and stuff happens in and to relationships. You and your partner are human beings. You are individuals. You evolve and you change. Your committed partnership or marriage is dynamic. Your relationship is not static; certain aspects of your partnership are sure to change. Nothing and no one ever remains the same. At some point in your relationship, you and/or your partner will change without a doubt. As a result, your relationship and certain characteristics of your partnership may need to be altered.

116

The Couples Cure™ Book, Mastering the Art of Relationships in 7 Easy Steps addresses two ways in which couples need to renegotiate. The first is a situational re-do. The second is to refresh, rejuvenate or reinvigorate your relationship.

Situational Re-Do

The opportunity to mend your relationship is called a *situational re-do*. A situational re-do can occur when all other aspects of your relationship are pretty much in order. This situational circumstance presents an opportunity to address and renegotiate the terms of your relationship around a particular issue.

For example, a partnership may experience difficulties with family, household responsibilities, dealing with in-laws and friends, job transitions, or any number of isolated challenges. On occasion, some aspect of your relationship may have deviated from the original understanding and you and/or your partner may be unhappy.

Not everything that is altered in a relationship requires a complete re-do. However, you and your partner are unique. Your relationship is one of a kind. There are circumstances that impact your union that will have no effect on you, your partner or your relationship. Nonetheless, there may be an occasion where you and your partner need to renegotiate, discuss, modify or change the terms of a prior relationship understanding or agreement. These occasions or periodic re-do needs are situational. The situational need for you and your partner to re-do a particular aspect of your relationship is one of the reasons Step 7, **Renegotiate** was written.

Renegotiate And Rejuvenate Your Relationship

The second reason for this chapter is to rejuvenate long-term relationships. If or when your relationship needs rejuvenation or reinvigorating, it provides the guidelines for a committed couple's relationship refresh or re-do. The circumstances I refer to here concern situations where couples have been in long-term relationships or committed partnerships. This chapter is also for those long-term relationships where a change has occurred. In this setting, both you and your partner know instinctively that something isn't quite right, or you are aware that something has changed in your relationship. Neither you nor your partner may be able to identify the source or why the change occurred. Yet, you both know that something should be discussed and done, even though you may not know what it is or how to tackle the problem.

There are many scenarios that are applicable under these circumstances. You may call it a couple's relationship refresh, a partner's renewal, a reinvigoration or rejuvenation of your partnership. These refresh scenarios are what I refer to as couples re-dos. Consider the reinvigorating look and feel of a fresh coat of paint on your home, or the pride you feel when you've just had an expensive detailed job for you car inside and out. What about a total personal make-over and how that makes you feel?.

Most relationships need to have refreshing makeovers from time to time. This chapter provides the easy process for you to re-do or renegotiate your solidly committed relationship.

It's Never Too Late To Renegotiate

To begin the renegotiate or re-do process, the first step is to take responsibility and ownership for your life and your part in your current relationship. You have to own and completely accept that the combination of your decisions and actions and your partner's decisions and actions had a direct impact on the current status of your relationship.

Whatever happened to your relationship in the past cannot be reversed; however, it does not necessarily have to continue. You and your partner can renegotiate new terms of your evolving relationship as you move forward. It's never too late to enhance the quality of your current partnership or make your relationship better. This is the time for you to let go of all the old baggage, beliefs and behaviors you've embraced for years. Chances are some of your old behaviors, deep-rooted beliefs and

118

attitudes no longer serve you. Some are simply unhealthy habits that you may have had for years. Now is not the place nor time to cut and paste your old baggage into the re-designed relationship you desire.

A healthy foundation to renegotiate any aspect of your partnership requires you and your partner to modify some beliefs, behaviors and actions. It is the combined beliefs, behaviors and actions that resulted in the current state of your relationship. Thus, modification of beliefs, behaviors and actions is necessary in the habit changing process to anchor new emotional and physical steps required to make changes. The rewards are well worth the effort.

The Renegotiate Process

> *MOTIVATION is what gets you started.*
>
> *HABIT is what keeps you going.*
>
> Author Unknown

To renegotiate and rejuvenate your relationship may best be described as a complete transformation of your relationship. It should be considered a transformation because the very foundation and fiber of how you interact with one another is about to change. Your behavior and actions (or lack of action) will dictate the nature of your relationship from this point forward. This chapter will help you mold your newly revived relationship so that you become the architect of your partnership and your life.

Transitions of any kind take courage. Couples who have the courage to stand up and fight for the partnership they truly want will survive. Those couples who are weak, don't have the conviction or cannot affirm with a *"Yes, I want to enhance this relationship"* may have difficulty with this chapter. The issue is not the chapter. The issue is really a question: Am I committed to having a healthy, fulfilling partnership?

I've seen far too many couples who were not willing to do the work required to save their relationship. Will you and your partner be one of the statistics in the category of couples that simply exist? Or will you and your partner face the challenge of working to make it the best relationship possible? I certainly hope the latter is the case!

The renegotiate process requires effort. It requires you and your partner to sit down and work through your plan to renegotiate. Following are two questions you and your partner may want to answer and one action item necessary to complete the renegotiate process:

Question 1. Am I willing to accept responsibility for my share in making the relationship what it is today?

- What have I done to contribute to the current state of affairs in my partnership?

- What kind of choices have I made?

- How have I communicated with my partner?

- Have I been respectful to my partner?

- Have I been sarcastic or condescending to my partner or the relationship?

- Have I intentionally or unintentionally sabotaged the relationship?

In order to begin the healing and growth process you must first accept responsibility for what you've contributed to the relationship – both positive and negative. Quite often partners are apprehensive about taking responsibility for fear of appearing weak or giving into their mate. So, there are those occasions when the ego simply takes over and causes you to behave in inappropriate ways. Understand that the ego, sarcasm and negativity have no place in a process to renegotiate the terms of your relationship and solve challenging problems you may have.

In one of my couples coaching sessions, I asked Bill to write a note to his partner, Beth, and make a list of those things that he felt responsible for in their relationship. The couple had spent the last few weeks not speaking. They were on "limited speaking terms" when one partner refused to talk with the other and the condition deteriorated into "the silent treatment." It was not uncommon for this couple to go sometimes as long as three weeks without extended conversation. I asked Bill, *"What value was derived from days and weeks without speaking to Beth?"* Unfortunately Bill could not give me a solid answer about the benefits for engaging in silent treatment behavior.

The following is an exact quote from Bill's note to Beth:

I take full responsibility for everything that you start;

I take responsibility for every argument you start;

For when you don't speak;

For not being rich enough to keep you in the lifestyle that you want;

For wanting to give love and be loved;

What was I thinking?

I agree with you that resolution can only happen if I learn to do what you want without challenging.

You win!

After reading the note, I asked Bill if he was serious about what he had written, or whether he was being funny or sarcastic. He replied, *"No, my note to Beth was not intended to be funny or sarcastic."* He said, *"I am quite serious about the note in terms of what my responsibilities in the demise of our relationship."*

What do you see as the culprit in the above quote from Bill? Do you recognize any problems with his apology? Has Bill truly taken responsibility for his actions or has he placed the blame on Beth? Can you hear and feel the sarcasm in Bill's tone? Do you really think that Bill was attempting to resolve the challenges in his relationship or was he merely looking to place all blame on Beth?

Unfortunately, Bill could not see or chose not to acknowledge any issues with his response. He could not see that sarcasm, insults and attacks on his partner have no place in the renegotiation process. In order for this couple to move forward, Bill needs to move beyond his attempt to protect his ego and place the blame on Beth. Interestingly enough, in other environments, Bill is a very charming and warm individual. He has a delightful personality and has a host of friends. However, when it comes to apologizing, Bill missed the mark.

Now, ask yourself about your own techniques when you apologize. Do you take responsibility for whatever the circumstances are in your state of affairs? Do you protect your ego, evade responsibility and place the blame on your partner? Words are powerful. Is your ego and pride worth sacrificing your relationship?

Question 2. Do I want to make my relationship work?

This is a yes or no question. If the answer to this question is anything other than *Yes* -- either on your part or that of your partner, you should be concerned. The reason for the concern is that when there is no definitive *Yes* to making the relationship work, the partner who is unable to answer *Yes* appears to lack conviction to improving the relationship. If you or your partner hesitate, won't or can't say *Yes*, that's a problem. The answer to that question has to be without hesitation and a *Yes* by both you and your partner. If there is apprehension, that could indicate a challenge for you or your partner. The reason you're apprehensive about saying *Yes* may be that you're concerned about being hurt. You may be worried about protecting your ego, looking weak, or appearing to be soft.

My challenge for both you and your partner is to stand tall, right now. I challenge both of you to make the commitment now to change the parameters of your relationship. If you don't make the commitment and your intentions are not fully vested, I guarantee that you'll be in the same spot a day from now or week from now, a month from now, and a year from now. The reason is that your intent, consciousness and behavior are what provide the driving force behind any change. If you keep doing the same things that you've been doing, you'll most likely continue to get the same results you've been getting.

By the time you get to this point, your relationship could be on shaky ground. I've talked with numerous couples who responded with *"I will if she/he will,"* when I asked the question about whether or not they want to make their relationship work.

I had two separate coaching sessions with a couple. I asked the wife if she wanted to and was willing to work through the challenges in this relationship. Her response was, *"Well, yes, only if he is".* When I asked her husband if he wanted to and was willing to work through the challenges of this relationship, his said, *"Things are alright as is."* Neither partner came forward with a resounding *"Yes, I am willing to do anything and everything necessary to improve our relationship and make it work for the two of us."*

What I've learned over the years is that most people are not willing to go down that path of "making themselves vulnerable" and therefore may lose perfectly good relationships.

The behavior of this husband and wife can be summed up in one word: fear! Both are afraid to emotionally invest in their relationship or to make themselves vulnerable. Rather than putting aside their ego and recommitting to do what is necessary to make their relationship work, they opt to do nothing. They choose not to commit to improving their partnership. Consequently, their relationship may end or remain unfulfilling for one or both partners. They may dissolve the relationship based on irreconcilable differences or they may continue to ignore areas of dissatisfaction. I call it absurdity. Perfectly good relationships end or continue to suffer because of fear. ***Don't let yourself and your partner become another relationship fatality based on fear!***

Now that you have answered the preceding questions, you are ready to take the actions required to complete the renegotiate process.

Action: Start with the End in Mind, Renegotiate and Make a Contract

Sit down with a piece of paper and pen and make a list of all the things and characteristics you want to be, see, do, and how you want to act in your renegotiated relationship. What does your renegotiated relationship look like?

Now is the time to literally make that list. This exercise involves the two of you.

First, you and your partner should make independent lists. Next, sit together and compare notes; then, finalize one list of changes on which you both agree. This process is no different than strategic planning in a business environment. It's very similar to examining the process for improving your sport team's chances of winning the championship. The same list is similar to what you prepare for weight loss or smoking cessation. The process is identical.

Make a list of what you want, your partner wants, and what your relationship will look like. Finally, be sure and address the obstacles and challenges that you may encounter. That too is part of your strategic partnership plan.

Be sure to write it down. This includes whatever you want, what you expect, and what the ultimate outcomes you desire. *If it's not in writing, it doesn't exist.*

> *"In a negotiation, we must find a solution that pleases everyone, because no one accepts that they must lose and that the other must win. Both must win!"*
>
> Nabil N. Jamal

Get together in a calm, civilized environment to share and discuss your wishes, expectations, and desired outcomes. Remain flexible and be willing to compromise so that you both end with a win-win situation. If necessary, go back to Chapter 4 — **The Message** and refresh your memory on how to communicate with your partner and then agree on the terms of your relationship.

Together you and your partner should review the list, make changes, and agree upon the terms of what will become your newly revised relationship contract. Throughout the renegotiate process, think, believe and act as though your relationship already has the qualities you've listed.

Stick to it! Even if you backslide, get back on the program. You'll find the benefits of a relationship redesign, after you and your partner renegotiate, is well worth the effort. This renegotiate process can be used at any time to re-do any aspects of your partnership to get the healthy, fulfilling relationship you deserve.

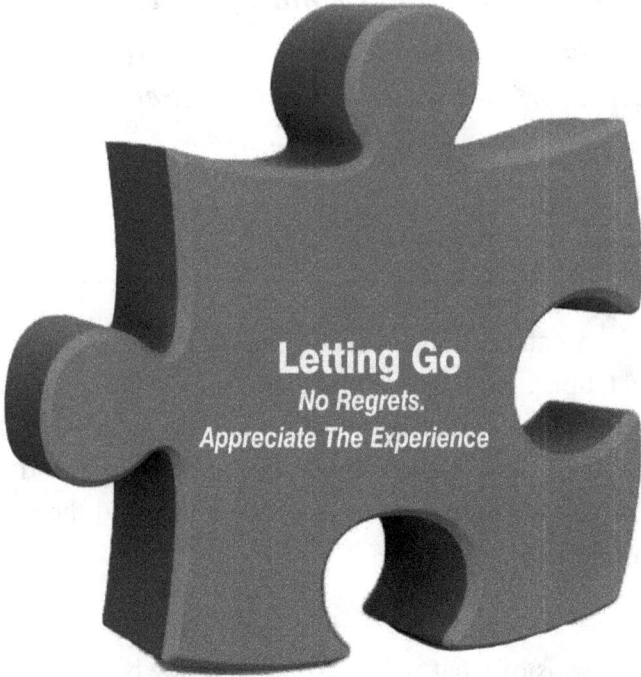

Letting Go
No Regrets.
Appreciate The Experience

Chapter 8: Letting Go

No Regrets. Appreciate The Experience.

> *Any action is often better than no action, especially if you have been stuck in an unhappy situation for a long time. If it is a mistake, at least you learn something, in which case it's no longer a mistake. If you remain stuck, you learn nothing.*
>
> Eckhart Tolle

This is Chapter 8 of *The Couples Cure™ Book, Mastering The Art of Relationships in 7 Easy Steps.* No, you didn't miscalculate. There is no mistake. The chapter numbers are labeled correctly. Yes, there are 9 chapters in this book and not 7.

The first 7 steps include fun and easy activities on **Self Knowledge** (Step 1), **Mindset** (Step 2), **Embracing Change** (Step 3), **The Message** (Step 4), **Platinum Sex Rule** (Step 5), **Money Mates** (Step 6) and **Renegotiate** (Step 7). These chapters were designed to inspire and motivate committed partners to embrace the formulas and wisdom of hundreds of individuals and couples who have healthy, fulfilling relationships. By embracing and applying their wisdom and experience, you too can master the art and science of relationships and learn to revitalize your own relationship with your partner.

Chapters 8, **Letting Go,** and Chapter 9, **Take Action Now**, are the final steps in *The Couples Cure™ System* and are as significant as Chapters 1 through 7. Chapter 8, **Letting Go**, provides the remedies for the very real situation if and when you and your partner must end your relationship. It offers you healthy choices and alternatives for letting go, having no regrets and appreciating the relationship experience. This chapter is about self-preservation when your relationship is ready for dissolution.

If you and your partner have already taken the path of reconciliation and opted to do everything within your powers to rejuvenate and rekindle your relationship, there is no need to continue reading Chapter 8. You should immediately move on to Chapter 9, **Take Action Now**. The final chapter of the book is a must read for everyone, regardless of the status of your relationship. **Take Action Now** outlines success strategies and provides a simple plan to help you achieve any goal related to your partnership or otherwise.

This Chapter, **Letting Go**, introduces guidance and support for individuals and couples who, after many weeks, months, sometimes years of struggle and conscientious effort, are simply unable to salvage their relationship. You and I would be foolish if we assumed that every couple that reads this book is able to renovate their relationship and live happily thereafter. We don't live in a fairy tale world. We know the statistics of broken relationships. If all relationships were salvageable, the average U.S. divorce rate would be significantly lower than the current 50% divorce rate for first time marriages, 67 % for second marriages and a whopping 74% for third marriages. Although recent theories indicate that first time marriages are on the decline in the U.S., I do not have hard statistics to present here, other than the fact that they are supposed to be on the decline.

In spite of the alleged decline of first-time marriages, divorce statistics are still high. Unfortunately, the data is often not available or inconsistent on long-term un-married and committed life partners, e.g., heterosexual and homosexual partners who are unmarried and live together, and other couples who commit themselves as life partners yet do not live together. Regardless of percentages or lack of data, painful human emotions often are the result of broken relationships.

There are several variations of the following quote, found in literature, where the word "misery" is substituted for "suffering". Nevertheless, the meaning is that in life and relationships we all experience pain. However, **we all have a choice when it comes to suffering**, which is self-inflicted and exacerbates the pain. The same holds true for separating or letting go of partnerships. What we wish to convey here is that there are steps you and your partner can take to avoid adding suffering or misery to the often difficult separation or letting go process.

Pain is inevitable.
Suffering is optional.

Haruki Murakami

Know that there are a large number of partnerships that end amicably. I know of at least two very intimate marriages that ended after 10 years and 23 years respectively. The spouses in both relationships get along fabulously now. They travel together, they have lived together and they consider one another their best friend. As a mater of fact, both of these divorced couples get along much better as ex-spouses than they ever did as married partners.

However, all break-ups are not that good natured, harmonious and friendly (although they can be). Unfortunately, a substantial number of severed relationships generate a lot of emotional turmoil caused by the break-up process, broken partnership, and/or divorce.

Trifecta Benefits Package

Chapter 8 delivers a trifecta benefit package designed to help you weather the emotional storm and turmoil that you can experience as a result of your intimate relationship breakup process.

The trifecta benefits or three golden nuggets place emphasis on:

- Acceptance
- Appreciation of the experience, and
- Self Preservation.

Acceptance. Far too often people equate acceptance with approval or being passive. Acceptance is not approval. Acceptance is simply an acknowledgement that a situation is the result of prior choices. Acceptance of a person is an acknowledgement of who they are just as they are, without judgment and without trying to fix or change them. In the case of an irreparable or broken relationship, acceptance allows you to deal with a situation and the person as they are and move on from anger and hurt.

When you accept a situation for what it is and individuals for who they are, you live your truth. The truth will set you free and allow you to let go.

Appreciation. In every experience and every relationship there are benefits. Sometimes the benefits are more difficult to see. Sometimes the benefits that reveal themselves are learning experiences. When you look at your relationship with the intention of appreciating the positive and learning experience, the benefits will be revealed. Sometimes the blessing is in the break-up. Have no regrets. Appreciate the experience, and let it go!

Self-Preservation. Self-preservation is the first law of nature. Protection, maintenance and love of and for your mind, body and spirit are essential to your survival and happiness. If you don't care about yourself, no one else will. You must cultivate the courage to stand in your own light and know beyond a shadow of a doubt that you are worthy of love and fulfillment regardless of breakups in your relationships.

> ### *Self-Preservation is the First Law of Nature*
>
> Samuel Butler

An Unworkable Relationship

Not all relationships are workable or can be repaired. Below is an example of one such relationship where the woman wanted to end the relationship and the man did not. They were both in their mid 40's, loved one another, but were unfortunately not the right fit for one another at that time.

Late one evening, I received a call from Toni. Toni had been referred by one of my coaching clients. Toni said, *"Hi Prestell, Stephanie told me that you were a couple's coach and that you might be able to help me."*

"What seems to be the problem?" I asked.

"It's my boyfriend, Sam," she said. *"Sam and I are always arguing."* After several personal clarifying questions, I asked Toni to tell me about their issues.

Toni goes on to say: *"Sam and I are constantly quarrelling. He wants the relationship, but I no longer want to be in the relationship."* She likes him but they argue a lot.

Toni had a number of other major concerns about Sam. She had issues with trusting him. Apparently he lied to her a number of times. She found out, confronted Sam about the lies and he later confessed to his untruths. He lacked the maturity of a 40-year-old man. Sam was financially unstable

131

and had no real job or source of income. In addition, there were a number of other instances when Toni expressed her disgust for Sam's irresponsible behavior.

Toni said Sam showed little or no follow through and had not accomplished much in his life.

Toni expressed a desire for a partner with whom she could look forward to a future and growing old together. She asked Sam if he had goals and a vision for himself and their life together. According to Toni, Sam had neither goals nor a vision.

She continued to say that Sam did not agree with her on anything on almost any topic. He simply argued with her for the sake of arguing. I could hear the fatigue in her voice. She was concerned that she'd have to push Sam, pull him or constantly urge him to improve his status in life.

Toni's assessment was that her relationship, for the most part, was dysfunctional. The dysfunction she referred to was applicable to almost every aspect of their partnership, especially as it related to Sam's untrustworthiness, lack of stability, immaturity and financial irresponsibility. All of these were issues that Toni was unwilling to continue working on or fix.

After listening to Toni and asking a number of value and behavioral questions, I asked Toni to answer the following:

1. Do you want the relationship? And are you willing to do what is required to rejuvenate the relationship?

2. What does your ideal relationship look like?

3. Is he capable, is he willing to work and meet you halfway to do what is required to achieve the kind of relationship you both want?

I requested that Toni make a list of the pros and cons about Sam. The pros would include all of the fun times, all the good things he does, and all the good feelings she has about him. The cons would include those things that irritate her, make her angry, and cause her to distrust him.

I let Toni know that if the answer to the first question is *Yes,* then there are challenges ahead. Her relationship can possibly be mended and put together again with major effort.

If, on the other hand, the answer to the first question is not a resounding *Yes*, perhaps she needs to consider letting go and moving on.

When To Let Go

Here's what I've discovered from the hundreds of individuals and couples who shared their experiences about relationships:

*   Not everyone is supposed to be in a committed relationship or married.

*   Just because you love someone does not mean they are good for you.

*   Sometimes you and your spouse, partner, lover are better off just being friends.

*   There are many people who are in love, but do not like each other. Liking your partner and considering him/her a friend are essential to a healthy fulfilling relationship. In other words, having a long term partnership with someone who you don't like or regard as a good friend may be difficult at best.

- Acceptance and forgiveness are more beneficial to you as a giver than to the recipient of your acceptance or forgiveness.

- When a break-up or divorce occurs, let it go. Have no regrets and appreciate the experience.

So, you ask, *"How do I know when it's time to let go?"* Perhaps the following poem will shed some light on this question.

When It's Time To Let Go – You Know

When it's time to let go – you know.
When it's time to let go – you know.

The difficulty lies in taking the action;
Even though you know your present situation lacks satisfaction.

Sometimes it just seems hard because you don't want the pain.
Ask yourself: Am I fulfilled in the current situation?
Is it worth the strain?

What typically occurs is accustomed familiarity.
Not joy, not fulfillment, merely habitual polarity.

Either way, it is not a sound nor healthy situation.
Query your heart and soul: Do I want the same circumstances
5 years from now? 10 years from now? 20 years from now?
The same continuation?

If the answer is No, you've got to let go.
If the answer is No. Then you've got to let go.

Too often you are afraid because you become conditioned
to accept less than you deserve.
When you know your partner has gotten on your very last nerve.

You know in your heart even without saying the part.
What's in the head is different than what's in the heart.

And if the answer is No. You've got to let go.
If the answer is No ... then you've got to let go!

Prestell Askia

135

Steps To Letting Go

If after all of your and your partner's efforts a decision is made to dissolve the relationship, the following steps will provide assistance in helping you work through this process.

Step 1. Acceptance. Accept your relationship as it is, not as you wish it to be.

Step 2. Appreciation. Assess the positive and the negative aspects of your relationship.

Step 3. Self-Preservation. Does my relationship increase my self-love and preserve my sense of self worth?

Step 4. Decide. Do you and/or your partner really wish to put in the hard work required to try and salvage your relationship?

Step 5. If the answer to the question in Step 4 is a resounding *Yes*, return to the beginning of this book and continue working on your relationship. In some instances, this may require assistance or counseling from a third party.

Step 6. If the answer to the question in Step 4 is a definite *No*, allow yourself to accept the relationship as it is, let go of your expectations and desires, and take action (see next chapter) to move forward.

> ***Remember:***
> In life and in relationships, pain is inevitable but suffering is your choice.

Step 7. Regardless of whether the answer to Step 4 is *Yes* or *No*, on occasion you and/or your partner may need additional help navigating the process of letting go. Even though you may not require a licensed clinician, psychologist or psychiatrist, you may want additional assistance. Know that confidential life and relationship coaching support and guidance is always available. Don't hesitate to contact *The Couples Cure Lady* for personal and group coaching services, training, and couples resources.

Take Action Now
It's Time

Chapter 9: Take Action Now

It's Time

> *Action is a great restorer and builder of confidence.*
> *Inaction is not only the result, but the cause, of fear.*
> *Perhaps the action you take will be successful;*
> *perhaps different action or adjustments will have to*
> *follow. But any action is better than no action at all.*
>
> Norman Vincent Peale

Final Piece In The Relationship Puzzle

The final piece of the relationship puzzle in *The Couples Cure™ Book, Mastering the Art of Relationships in 7 Easy Steps* is to **Take Action Now**. This last act is as critical to your success in a healthy, fulfilling relationship as the original 7 easy steps. This final piece of the relationship puzzle allows you to move forward and implement the changes you want to see as a result of your newfound knowledge about yourself and your relationship. **Take Action Now** also helps guide you and your partner, the architects of your relationship, through the transformation process as you begin to put the finishing touches on your newly designed partnership.

Your Relationship Primer

Your thought-provoking journey through this book should be considered your partnership primer. This journey has introduced you to new concepts and fresh processes about how to improve your relationship. You've had an opportunity to learn from the wisdom of hundreds of discussions with individuals and couples who shared the critical elements of healthy, happy and fulfilled partnerships. You've also been the beneficiary of conversations about what not to do in, to and with your relationship.

This book has guided you through a series of relationship puzzle pieces. These puzzle pieces are reflected in the first seven chapters as the *7 Easy Steps in Mastering the Art of Relationships*. These 7 steps represent the partnership factors that are essential to enhance and improve your relationship.

You've had an opportunity to indulge yourself and learn more about who you really are through the enlightening chapter on **Self Knowledge**. Next you opened the door to the power of attitude and intention with **Mindset**. **Embracing Change** helped you appreciate that nothing ever stays the same, not you, your life, your environment and certainty not your relationship. These are all in a state of flux and constantly changing. Your task was to appreciate and value each occasion when you encountered change as a Rise of the Phoenix opportunity. You also learned the delicate nuances of Loving Communications, The Morse Code of Relationships in **The Message** Chapter. Ensuring both partners are recipients of sensual, intimate Win-Win Sex was the over arching message delivered in **The Platinum Sex Rule**. **Money Mates,** The Couples Guide to Easy Finances, helped to bring financial balance to your partnership. The chapter titled **Renegotiate** spells out the strategy and tactics for minor or major redesign, restructure or complete make over of your relationship, whenever it is Time For A Re-Do.

Finally, Chapter 8 on **Letting Go** is a realistic, practical and civilized guide for those partners who ultimately end up severing their relationship. It is a progressive approach to separation or divorce. The breakup is the blessing for both partners; this tolerant approach enables each partner to leave with *No Regrets* while they *Appreciate The Experience* they shared together.

What Now?

According to Tommy Lasorda, there are three kinds of people in the world:
People Who Make Things Happen,
People Who Watch What Happens, and
People Who Wonder What Happened.

Question: Which kind of person are you?

If you're sincerely conscientious about improving your relationship, you've gathered a lot of information from this book thus far. The question is what to do with all that data. You want to take the next step. You want to improve and enhance your partnership. You certainly don't want to be filled with knowledge yet do nothing with the information you've acquired. Worse yet, you continue to complain and do nothing to change your circumstances. Shame on you if you let yourself fall into a *do nothing* partner category!

If you know that something needs to be done, this is the time to **Take Action Now**! Chances are you also know that you will more than likely be the partner who initiates the change. After all, you have to be the change you want to see.

Now is the time! There are three actions yet to complete. Get clarity, imagine what you want your future relationship to look and feel like, and **Take Action Now**.

> *"Change the way you look at things*
>
> *and the things you look at change."*
>
> Wayne W. Dyer

Get Clarity

When you are perfectly clear about what you want, the outcome is easier to attain. The more clarity you and your partner have about the changes you want to see in your relationship, the more likely you are to realize those changes. Clarity enables you to identify what changes are important and eliminate all the nonessentials. Clarity of actions required to enhance and improve your relationship will enable you to establish and execute your partnership priorities with laser sharp precision.

How much time do you spend on research and getting clarity on material purchases, looking at new car reviews, comparing furniture styles, getting a dog or cat, considering where you want to live?

You spend hours if not days planning for a special dinner party that you host during the Thanksgiving Holiday season. Questions and preparation like when to have the party, who to invite, the party theme, menu, seating arrangement, whether to serve white or red wine. You want to make sure that everything about the party is flawless. All this planning for the party takes a fair amount of research, planning, coordination and effort.

Also recall the occasions when you and your partner spent time planning a two week vacation to the Caribbean Islands. You drooled over where you wanted to go, which location was best, the daily excursions you wanted to take and how to make sure you saw everything on your vacation to-do list. It sometimes took days or even months to plan a mere two-week vacation.

Think about the process you go through when you decide to repaint your room or home? Reflect on all the effort and research before you selected several colors to consider. You wanted a soft cream paint color to coordinate with your eclectic décor. Selecting a simple soft cream color was a difficult task. There were so many shades of cream in the color family. You had to consider ivory, warm cream, beige, white, off white, light tan, Navaho white, sand, bone, too many other options — all in the soft cream color pallet. You took numerous trips to the local home stores to get color strips. You then taped the color strips to the wall to get a feel for what the color looked like in your home with your furniture and your lighting. Once you decided on the top three colors, you returned to the store to get actual paint samples; then, went home, and painted color blocks of the three finalist colors on the wall. Was there too much red or blue tint in the soft cream color? Was the color rich enough or was it too pale? Did your selected color offer a combined primer and paint for a one coat application? Did the color you picked dry darker than you anticipated? Did that color pair well with others for a homogeneous color scheme for the room? So many options, choices to make and effort required.

After all, selecting a paint color requires serious consideration. That paint color is a reflection of you and you'll live with that color for a long time. Therefore, it has to be just right; and if that process requires weeks of deliberation to select the right color, so be it!

Hopefully you got the message from the above example. The time spent on vacations, pets, dinner parties, paint color, new cars and home purchases sometimes far outweighs the time you and your partner spend thinking about, discussing and planning what to do and how to enhance your relationship.

The questions for you and your partner to ask are:

- What amount of time do we spend planning and getting clarity about how we'd like to see our relationship enhanced?

- Do my partner and I have a plan or a vision of what we want our relationship to look like?

- Do my partner and I seriously weigh all the options and ways to make our partnership better?

If you and your partner don't put any effort into your relationship, how is it then that you think your relationship will improve? Seriously now, if you don't make the effort and commitment, nothing about your relationship will change for the better.

Imagine What You Want

> *Vision without action is fantasy;*
> *action without a vision is chaos.*
>
> Rev. Michael Bernard Beckwith

Regardless of where you are in your relationship, it's never too late to make improvements. Change is always possible with effort. Now that you're equipped with the magic formula from *The Couples Cure™ Book, Mastering the Art of Relationships in 7 Easy Steps*, imagine what you want from your partnership. Imagine and envision what you want for yourself. You and your partner should create a vision about what your ideal relationship will look and feel like. Then the two of you can take the action, do what is necessary to get the partnership you want.

> *Success comes from taking the initiative and following up ... persisting ... eloquently expressing the depth of your love.*
>
> *What simple action could you take today to produce a new momentum toward the success in your life?*
>
> Tony Robbins

Below, Tony Robbins eloquently identifies what it takes to be successful.

Success Strategy Detours

The real challenge is establishing and maintaining initiative, follow up, persistence, and expressing the depth of your love to produce momentum toward success in your life.

Before we explore *The Couples Cure™ System* **Action Plan,** it is mandatory that we address the reasons people are frequently not successful in reaching their goals and dreams. What I know for sure is that staying the course to reach or complete your goals is sometimes more problematic than you anticipate. In the past, you may have experienced a road to your success that was laced with trials and tribulations you were not able to overcome. Or you may have encountered challenges along your success route you were not prepared to tackle and therefore fell short of your goals. I've been there and done that. I know how frustrating it can be.

The difficulties and shortcomings on the road to success are exactly why I highlight them now. I want you to be prepared. When you acknowledge an issue and deal with it before it has a chance to disrupt your success plan, the better you are prepared to combat and overcome those issues and challenges. Here are some of the reasons you may fail to reach or complete your goals:

- You fail to clarify your goals.
- Your goals are not written down.
- You don't know what you want or want it strongly enough.
- Your goals are unrealistic or to too difficult.
- You're not persistent in pursing your goals.
- You don't follow up.
- You have no accountability.
- You don't have a support system.

The Action Plan

If you want your relationship to improve, an action plan is essential. Unless you and your partner have a plan and take action, the relationship will remain the same. So, create your plan and then **ACT**.

Action
Changes
Things

To help you through the final steps in your journey with *The Couples Cure™ Book, Mastering the Art of Relationships in 7 Easy Steps*, it is my pleasure to share another golden nugget from my training seminars. This nugget was developed for The Askia Group's *Success Strategies Seminar*. After years of courses, workshops and books, I was unable to find one comprehensive goal setting form. I was looking for a form that could be used by my students to track and provide a simple overview of their tasks and goals. Necessity is the mother of invention.

On the next page is a copy of the Action Plan from my *Success Strategies Seminar*; adapted for *The Couples Cure™ System*.

The Action Plan is divided into quadrants, and labeled as follows:

- Upper Left = Current Status or What's Lacking, What Needs Improvement
- Upper Right = Ideal Future, Completed Goal, or Vision
- Lower Left = What Needs To Be Done, How You Plan To Do It
- Lower Right = When? Your Time frame? Be Specific.

To make it easy and ensure you understand how to complete the Action Plan, a sample action plan is provided for two of the seven steps, **Self Knowledge** and **Platinum Sex Rule**. On the sample action plan, the upper left quadrant shows the current status. The upper right quadrant shows what the ideal future looks like. The bottom left quadrant reflects the actions required to accomplish the goals. Finally, the bottom right quadrant shows a specific date or time frame vital to accomplish the goals. Also for your convenience, an 8 ½" x 11" PDF copy of *The Couples Cure™ System Action Plan* is available for download on The Couples Cure™ Book.com.

Now it's your and your partner's job to complete your own customized Action Plan. When developing this customized action plan, you'll need to complete all seven steps: **Self-Knowledge, Mindset, Embracing Change, The Message, The Platinum Sex Rule, Money Mates, and Renegotiate**. Now, you and your partner are ready to begin your relationship transformation process.

Sample Action Plan for Self Knowledge and Platinum Sex Rule

Current Status	Future: What I Want To Accomplish
✧ **Self Knowledge:** *Not living my values*	✧ **Self Knowledge:** *Live in harmony with my values*
✧ Mindset	✧ Mindset
✧ Embracing Change	✧ Embracing Change
✧ The Message	✧ The Message
✧ **Platinum Rule Sex:** *Not engaging in Win-Win Sex*	✧ **Platinum Rule Sex:** *Enjoy Win-Win Sex*
✧ Money Mates	✧ Money Mates
✧ Renegotiate	✧ Renegotiate
What Needs To Be Done	**When: Time Frame, Specific Date**
✧ **Self Knowledge:** *Complete Value Assessment* *Call Prestell for coaching help*	✧ **Self Knowledge:** *November 30* *December 1*
✧ Mindset	✧ Mindset
✧ Embracing Change	✧ Embracing Change
✧ The Message	✧ The Message
✧ **Platinum Rule Sex:** *Finish/discuss Partner Worksheets* *Start practicing Win-Win Sex*	✧ **Platinum Rule Sex:** *November 20* *December 1*
✧ Money Mates	✧ Money Mates
✧ Renegotiate	✧ Renegotiate

Fail-Safe Success Safety Nets & Support

Throughout your thought-provoking journey of mastering your relationship puzzle, I identified the challenges you might face on your road to achieving success. You are to be commended for following the guidelines and completing the fun exercises in *The Couples Cure™ Book, Mastering the Art of Relationships in 7 Easy Steps.* You have clarified your goals. You have completed your Action Plan. You have detailed where you now are in your partnership, where you want your relationship to be, what you have to do to achieve your goals, and when you intend to complete each of your actions.

The next stage is to speak to the solutions and safety nets you'll need in the event you encounter problems staying on track and achieving the goals on your *Action Plan.* You need to have a method for follow up to ensure you're on target at all times. You need to identify someone who will help you be responsible and personally accountable for your goals. And finally, you'll need a confidential support system that allows you to be completely honest, without judging you as you continue your relationship journey.

It can be uncomfortable at times to confide in your relatives about the partnership and marriage issues. Furthermore, if you speak negatively about your partner, later reconcile and forgive him or her, your relatives are not always as forgiving. Most of the time, your relatives are concerned first and foremost about you. Frequently, you only tell your relatives what you want them to know because you may be looking for empathy and sympathy during difficult times. Your family may not know the *whole story;* they may be less likely to forgive your partner.

Asking a good friend to function as an accountability partner for your most intimate relationship details can be embarrassing and may not be appropriate. You may only feel safe when discussing your discrete relationship details with someone who is impartial and can listen and understand your situation.

You want the very best for yourself and your relationship. I also want the very best for you and your relationship and recognize your need for complete confidentiality. Know that I understand your desire for privacy and a safe environment to discuss your most intimate feelings and experiences. These are reasons TheCouplesCureBook.com and *The Couples Cure™ Lady* are available with resources to help you through your partnership journey. Our coaching practice will provide the support you need. We will function as your accountability partner and success coach to help you reach your relationship goals. Don't hesitate to contact us for a host of couples options that can assist you with your relationship puzzle.

Keeping The Relationship You Deserve

Remember that all relationships, especially those as intimate and important as marriage or partnerships, require nurturing. In this context, nurturing means caring for and encouraging the growth or development of or tending to yourself, your partner, and your relationship. From very minor issues that arise frequently to more major ones that sometimes threaten the continuance of your relationship, each issue deserves your and your partner's attention. Based on my experience working with couples, the sooner you address small and large issues the more fulfilling and happy will be your relationship.

Also remember that all couples (and all other types of relationships) have their ups and downs and need to adapt to life's changes. Rather than dreading or fearing change, may you and your partner embrace change and work together to enjoy the fruits of your relationship as you recognize and adapt to change.

Finally, continue to refer to and use *The Couples Cure™ Book, Mastering the Art of Relationships in 7 Easy Steps* as a reference guide to keep the puzzle pieces of your relationship together and enjoy the relationship you so deserve!

My wish for you and your partner is to:

> *Laugh Often.*
>
> *Live With Gusto.*
>
> *Love With Passion!*
>
> Prestell Askia
> *The Couples Cure Lady*

HERE'S TO YOUR SUCCESS!

www.ingramcontent.com/pod-product-compliance
Lightning Source LLC
Chambersburg PA
CBHW072251270326
41930CB00010B/2341